GREAT NAVAL BATTLES: 2

BATTLE OF THE
CORAL SEA

CHRIS HENRY

GREAT NAVAL BATTLES: 2

BATTLE OF THE
CORAL SEA

CHRIS HENRY

NAVAL INSTITUTE PRESS
Annapolis, Maryland

First published in Great Britain in 2003 by Compendium Publishing, 43 Frith Street, Soho, London, W1D 4SA

Published and distributed in the United States of America and Canada by Naval Institute Press, 291 Wood Road, Annapolis, Maryland 21402-5034

Library of Congress Control No. 2003101569

ISBN 1 59114 033 1

PREVIOUS PAGE: **Douglas SBD Dauntlesses on USS *Enterprise*, April 11, 1942.**

Acknowledgments

The Author and Publisher thank the following for their help in putting this book together:

Artwork: (maps and color material) Jan Suermondt
Design: Tony Stocks
Editorial: Ilios Publishing
Printed In Hong Kong through Printworks International Ltd.

The photographs are from the Author's Collection or from the U.S. National Archives. The latter were researched by John Gressham. It is worth noting that the quality of some of the photographs is poor: illustrating long-distance naval battles, which often took place in bad light or weather conditions, is not conducive to great photography.

Contents

Introduction

It is hard to believe that an area such as the Coral Sea was ever the scene of a cataclysmic battle. The Solomon Islands and the coasts of Papua New Guinea are more suited to the tranquil lifestyles of the indigenous peoples than as the backdrop to one of the most dramatic naval battles of World War II. For the first time in a battle at sea no large-bore guns roared out and no battleship opposed another. It was the naval aviators and their machines that dealt out death and destruction. The Battle of the Coral Sea is still in some ways overshadowed by the major encounters that punctuate the Pacific War such as Midway, which took place almost immediately afterwards and seems to have been endlessly studied. Yet the Coral Sea is probably the more interesting of the two as it illustrates what happens when two roughly equal sides with similar technology fought a battle for which there was no known precedent. One author describes both sides as groping in the dark and this is certainly the feeling gained from an analysis of the events.

The great naval and amphibious war between America and Japan that raged across the Pacific Ocean during the early period of World War II could justifiably be described as the final act that settled a period of Japanese and US enmity. The roots of this conflict lie before World War II and were the result of the extension of competing spheres of influence. With hindsight, it seems inevitable that the economic juggernaut that was America would smother its opponent in the end, but in 1941 this was not at all clear and the Americans started the war on the back foot.

In the early 1930s The Japanese military had become increasingly involved in politics and by the time of the attack on Pearl Harbor had control over the government of Japan. The Japanese desire to control Asia was both racially and economically motivated. The fundamental driving force was a perceived need for living space and economic stability. Japan was a heavily populated country with few natural resources and these two elements, along with a belief in the racial superiority of the nation, developed into the concept of the Greater Asian Co-Prosperity sphere announced by Prime Minister Matsuoka Yôsuke in August 1940. The Japanese envisioned the Co-Prosperity Sphere as a bloc of Asian nations led by the Japanese and free from the influence of the Western powers. In common with Nazi Germany, Japan was prepared to invade other countries to bolster its own regime, using the resources and populations of invaded countries to sustain itself. In reality, there was no "co-prosperity" and the invaded and dominated nations under Japanese control were forced to do their bidding, supplying workers and resources with no benefit to themselves and suffering extreme privation in the process.

The invasion of China in July 1937, with the subsequent move into French Indo-China in 1940, persuaded the

ABOVE: New .50-cal. ammunition for this Grumman F4F Wildcat. The F4F was armed with six machine guns and achieved a high kill rate thanks to its sturdy construction.

LEFT: The Japanese aircraft carrier *Zuikaku* was launched in 1939. She and her sister *Shokaku* were badly mauled during the Battle of the Coral Sea and missed the crucial Battle of Midway because of this.

U.S. that the Japanese were not constrained by their opinions. The Japanese claim was that as an Island nation they had no raw materials, and in some respects it held true. Furthermore, the oil embargo placed on Japan by the U.S. since their intervention in China had exacerbated the supply situation. The army controlled the government and the army saw this as a threat. From this point onwards an increasing emphasis was placed upon an advance across the Pacific. Japan's Navy was young but experienced; it had won two great naval victories during the lifetime of the Imperial Navy. Between 1894 and 1905 the Chinese and the Russians had both been severely defeated at sea by the Imperial Japanese Navy.

The initial surprise Japanese attack at Pearl Harbor in 1941 dealt a savage blow to the U.S. Navy at its most important base. When this was combined with the destruction of British and Dutch naval elements in the region the Japanese genuinely looked as if they could dominate all of the Southeast Asia. It seems clear that they intended to subsume the ex-colonial provinces and then sue for peace. Thus the scene was set for a war that was fought across the length and breadth of the Pacific Ocean. Islands became fortresses and some of the most inhospitable places on earth became battlegrounds. In terms of naval forces the Japanese and Americans were roughly equal at the beginning of the war, though the Japanese had ten aircraft carriers in the Pacific in 1941 compared to the Americans' three. Aircraft were essential for this new kind of warfare and the Japanese had double the number of carrier-based aircraft and at least 400 more land-based aircraft than the allies. Were they to stretch themselves too thinly over the Pacific this advantage would be lost. That is why the carrier battles of the Coral Sea and Midway were critical to Japan's war effort and they had to be victorious in them both. Many works on the Battle of the Coral Sea have admirably dealt with the combat in the air, so this study attempts to redress the balance by covering other aspects of the battle in more detail. As more and more Japanese sources are translated one would hope that their accounts of the air defense of their ships would come to light as this author has yet to find a comprehensive account of the gunnery activities of the Japanese cruisers and destroyers.

RIGHT: Japan was one of the world's great naval powers—in the 1922 Washington Naval Treaty she was allowed to build three capital ships to every five built by the U.S. or Great Britain. By 1942 the Imperial Japanese Navy had more carriers—ten—than either of the big two, all of them equipped with first class equipment and highly trained crew. This is a construction scene from 1939.

Context

Naval warfare at the time

All the great seafaring nations of the world were convinced that the capital ship was the decisive weapon in naval warfare. The battles of Tsushima (1904) and Jutland (1916) were large naval engagements that were decided by the weight of shell provided by battleships. Or at least that was what many naval commentators led the services to believe. Even the Japanese Navy, who were to become the arch exponents of the torpedo bomber, were convinced that a grand naval battle in the traditional style between the Americans and themselves was inevitable. The evidence for this is irrefutable when one considers that they exhausted a great deal of time and resources building the super-battleships *Yamato* and *Musashi*.

The key date from when the two adversaries took divergent paths was 1921. Until that date Britain was an ally of Japan and it was the Washington Naval Treaty of 1922 that attempted to regulate the western and eastern spheres of influence. The Washington Naval Conference was one of the first ever attempts to limit arms expansion and it clearly marks how much weight all the world's great powers put on naval forces. As a result of this treaty, as well as the London naval treaty of 1930, Japan was only allowed a 6:10 ratio in capital ships in relation to the U.S. Navy. Concerned by the strategic limitations imposed on them, particularly by the restriction in the number of capital ships, the Japanese Navy sought other methods to redress the balance, in particular the wholesale adoption of the aircraft carrier. By 1941, Admiral Isoroku Yamamoto had nine carriers under his control and the Japanese had put their faith in naval airpower. In the first quarter of the 20th century the pioneers of air bombing were a vocal minority. The American pioneer Billy Mitchell had demonstrated as early as 1919 that airpower could seriously damage ships. Despite their success at Pearl Harbor the Japanese still considered that the decisive battle would be between conventional naval forces. The Battle of the Coral Sea would change all that. For the first time two carrier fleets without battleships fought each other without ever seeing each other directly, except through the eyes of their aviators. Naval aircraft and land-based aircraft carried out all the reconnaissance and delivered the killing blows. As such, it is hardly surprising that neither side knew how to deal with the problems of location and identification. That being said, the Japanese had amassed a vast amount of experience in a relatively short time. Following Pearl Harbor in December 1941, Japanese aircraft sank the British battleship the *Prince of Wales* and her supporting battle cruiser the *Repulse*. This attack was another indication to the Japanese that the aerial torpedo could be a battle-winning weapon. By January 1942, Japanese submarines had begun operating in the Indian Ocean, penetrating the inner sanctum of the once-invulnerable British Empire. The USS *Saratoga* also was torpedoed south of Hawaii in another blow to American prestige. In February 1942, the U.S. destroyers *Marblehead* and *Houston* were attacked in the Madoera Straight near Bali and by the end of the month the Battle of the Java Sea had been fought between the Japanese and the combined American, British and Dutch fleet. The Allies lost two

cruisers, three destroyers and the aircraft transport *Langley*. In fact by the end of February 1942, Allied forces had lost control of the seas around Java and the Japanese were pushing forward on all fronts. Probably more significant was the raid by the Japanese First Air Fleet into the Indian Ocean on March 28, 1942. For the British Far Eastern fleet this was too much and they begin a systematic search for the intruders. Running low on fuel they were quickly recalled but sortied from Addu atoll and were attacked by the Japanese First Air Fleet. The First Air Fleet also attacked Columbo, Sri Lanka (Ceylon), and sank a destroyer and an auxiliary cruiser as well as the cruisers *Cornwall* and *Dorsetshire*. On April 9, 1942, the First Air Fleet destroyed merchant shipping and raided into the Bay of Bengal. The British Far Eastern fleet was effectively removed from the area in a tacit acceptance of the power of the Japanese Navy. This catalog of success illustrates how efficient the Japanese Navy and Naval air arm had become.

Strategies and the coming struggle

Only two years after the end of the Russo-Japanese conflict the Japanese were planning to defeat the United States militarily by capturing the Philippine Islands and Guam. These islands had been won for the Americans through the

ABOVE LEFT: By 1942 naval theorists were beginning to realize that the aircraft carrier was the key to naval warfare and that the days of the big-gun battleship were numbered.

LEFT: An F4F prepares for take-off on *Lexington*. A twin 5in. DP mount can be seen in the background.

LEFT: U.S. seapower ensured that the Japanese were incapable of stopping amphibious assaults with seapower, and had to defend their territory on the ground. This is Okinawa, 1945.

RIGHT: USS *Yorktown*, CV-5, at sea, during 1942. Smaller than the Lexington class, *Yorktown* and sister ship *Enterprise* carried more aircraft. *Yorktown* was Rear-Adm. Fletcher's flagship at the Coral Sea.

BELOW RIGHT: Silhouette of a Douglas SBD.3 bomber. Success at the Coral Sea and Midway ensured that over 5,000 SBD Dauntlesses were built during the war.

defeat of Spain in the 1898 war and by capturing them the Japanese intended to provoke the Americans into sending a naval expeditionary force to recapture them. By doing this they would expose themselves to a Japanese attack, which, in the eyes of the Japanese planners, would give them the opportunity to strike when and where they wanted. This was expected to be somewhere near Japan, as this would ensure long American supply lines and Japanese short ones. All of this was thrown into confusion by the Washington Naval Treaty, but the Japanese still intended to keep the basic battle plan prior to World War II, except that they now needed to offset the obvious American superiority in ships.

The answer lay in the use of new weapons of war that would act as force multipliers. The aircraft, the torpedo and the submarine would all be used to destroy the American ships. If the Japanese could whittle down the American fleet by submarine and then aircraft attack, they would then be able to bring the depleted fleet to battle near Japan. The revised plan required new weapons and training techniques to be developed and the Japanese approached the task with relish. By the late 1930s the Japanese naval air arm was an outstanding example of a service that had been created relatively quickly but was extremely efficient.

As the United States acquired dependencies in the Pacific, so the question of how to defend them against an Asian threat was raised. War plan Orange was the plan that

laid out how the U.S. would defend against a Japanese attack, and it required that the Philippine Islands be defended until the U.S. Navy arrived to reclaim them. The Philippine Islands were 7,000 miles away from mainland America so it was predictable that any plan would require a large effort on the part of the navy. By the time war arrived, these plans had been altered and refined so that Orange became subsumed in the Rainbow series of war plans. Each Rainbow plan considered ways to protect the U.S. from attack depending upon what forces were available. Rainbow 3 assumed that the United States and the Western Hemisphere north of a latitude of ten degrees south was secure. The Philippines had no real naval base from which to operate and the army few land forces to defend the islands: there were about 17,000 men set against a Japanese invasion force roughly three times the size. Pearl Harbor was the largest naval base in the Pacific but it was 5,000 miles away from the Philippines. Rainbow 3 accepted that these men were to hold the islands until the U.S. Navy could arrive to relieve them. This task was complicated by the fact the Japanese had bases—the Marianas, Marshall and Caroline Islands—from which to sortie along the American supply route. Even as late as 1938 the Orange plan was being refined, but mention of the relief of the islands became more and more vague. Finally, it was decided that the operation was to go through a number of phases that meant the navy would progress across the Pacific rather than head directly for the islands.

The Japanese eventually decided to strike first and attempted to destroy the U.S. fleet at Pearl Harbor in 1941. After a victorious campaign on land and at sea they controlled effectively what they had thought of as the Greater Asia Co-prosperity sphere. Once this area had been occupied the Japanese began to worry about their defensive perimeter. Early raids by the U.S. Navy against the Japanese on the Northern and Southern Marshall Islands as well as Wake Island accentuated this feeling of unease amongst Japanese commanders. Both the USS *Yorktown* and the *Lexington* were used in this way to probe the Japanese and give American morale a boost. But it was in the area of New Guinea where the Japanese were beginning to entrench themselves and at Rabaul on the island of New Britain where they were determined to make a major depot and air base. The conquest of New Guinea was important to the Japanese and surprisingly Australia had become almost as important due to its strategic nature. To the Allies Australia was on the flank of their defense, to the Japanese it represented security for their gains and they intended to have it. Nevertheless the first stage of that progression was the capture of Port Moresby in the early part of 1942. Port Moresby was the principal land base in New Guinea on its south coast and Japanese land forces had been unable to capture it. New Guinea was vital as a pivot for Japanese defensive interests because it formed part of the perimeter they were expecting to hold.

Early attacks in March 1942 had affected the Japanese landing on the north coast of the island and the Japanese knew that they would have to hold the port on the south coast to have any chance of defending the area. It was also considered by them that the capture of the base would either act as a springboard for the invasion of Australia or act as an air base that would allow them to control the eastern seaboard of Australia. The plan that was finally adopted was to control any flow of weapons and supplies to Australia and Port Moresby was well situated for this. The Japanese considered endless strategic plans, but the concept of a decisive battle continued to be dominant. Yamamoto, the final arbiter in such matters, was convinced that a decisive battle at Midway was essential to deal the Americans a blow from which they could not recover. Clearly the longer the war went on the easier was for the United States to marshal its colossal economic and industrial power to defeat Japan. The Doolittle raid on April 18 changed everyone's perspective. On that day 16 B-25 bombers flew off the U.S. carrier *Hornet* and traveled 650 miles to drop bombs on Tokyo and other targets. Damage to the city was insignificant, but it was a major blow to Japanese prestige. The inability of military leaders to defend their homeland brought a sense of shame upon the high command.

So the decision to attack Port Moresby and then occupy it was worked up into a complex plan of attack in

RIGHT AND FAR RIGHT: Striking back! On April 1, 1942, 16 B-25s took-off from USS *Hornet* and raided Japan. Commanded by James (latter Lt. Gen.) Doolittle who received a Medal of Honor for the raid, the military effects were negligible. Strategically, however, it was a master stroke that improved U.S. morale and sent an icy wave of apprehension through Japanese ranks.

which several phases were required. Operation MO, as it was known, was composed of several different forces all intended to carry out specific tasks at specific times. Principally there was a transport force to move the Japanese soldiers to the other side of New Guinea. This included the supply vessels and transport vessels. A second invasion force was needed to take over the island of Tulagi in the Solomons, which had a suitable anchorage and would enable the Japanese to set up a naval airbase that could be used for reconnaissance and further attacks on the Coral Sea if needed. A third support force was to set up advanced airbases in the Louisade Archipelago and Santa Isabel. In order to protect and support the invasion force the Japanese provided a substantial group of cruiser and destroyers furthermore there would be a support group of one small aircraft carrier, four cruisers, one destroyer and one tanker for the invasion. A separate carrier force known as the striking force was to counterbalance any American task force at sea and consisted of two large carriers and supporting craft. Reconnaissance was to be carried out by seven submarines and there was a land based aircraft element that was intended to support the whole where possible. It should be noted that while all of this was happening preparations for the big Midway battle were being made so there was no question of the forces of one operation being reused at the other. In fact Midway took place almost immediately after the close of the Coral Sea operation and was probably the most significant sea battle of the Pacific campaign.

The Americans knew some kind of move was in the offing when Japanese force began concentrating at Rabaul. The Americans had carried out several raids into Japanese territory and were aware of Japanese activity in the New Guinea area. Their intention to attack Port Moresby was confirmed by intelligence gathered from intelligence intercepts and the U.S. commander Adm. Nimitz knew something had to be done. Considering that two of America's five carriers were now in the West Pacific having taken part in the Doolittle raid. It was the *Lexington* and the *Yorktown* that were chosen to form the nucleus of the fleet that would oppose any attempt on Port Moresby and Australia. What followed was search for sufficient cruiser and destroyers to support the Task Force. In fact Nimitz went further than just organizing the attack force. He also decided that the two carriers returning from the Pacific raid, namely the *Hornet* and *Enterprise*, should be included in the battle if they arrived at the area of operations in time. Admiral Halsey, who was in charge of the two carriers, was first required to put in at Pearl Harbor and then sail the 3,500 miles to the Coral Sea. They did not arrive anywhere near the islands until May 11, three days after the battle. Nevertheless they still presented a threat to the Japanese, as shall be seen.

The commanders

The first ever carrier against carrier engagement was played under the overall command of two of the great naval strategists of World War II: Admirals Nimitz at Pearl Harbor, and Yamamoto on board the Yamato at Truk. However, the real characters in the drama were Admirals Fletcher and Fitch on the American side, and Admirals Inoue, Goto and Takagi for the Japanese.

The U.S. Navy

At the top of the American tree was Admiral Chester W. Nimitz the Commander-in-Chief of the Pacific Fleet based at Pearl Harbor. Although Nimitz was in overall charge most of the decisions in the field were made by Rr. Adm. Frank J. Fletcher, who was the Commander-in-Chief of the naval and air forces during the battle.

As with many American naval commanders, Frank Jack Fletcher had graduated from the Naval Academy at Annapolis in 1906 and was a veteran of the invasion of Veracruz, Mexico, in 1914. His was to be the task to lead the very first American all-carrier battle. Early in 1941 he was commander of the *Yorktown* task force so he had already had some experience of fighting the Japanese in and around New Guinea. He has been described as a non-dynamic naval officer yet he fought in three major carrier battles in the Pacific and won all of them. It is clear that Nimitz had faith in him and this faith turned out to be justified. Fletcher was cautious when he needed to be but also took risks, which is a prerequisite of any commander at this level of conflict.

Aubrey W. Fitch was another graduate from Annapolis and was considered to be an air specialist, so he took over all air operations when the battle started. In 1930, Fitch went through training to become a naval aviator, and throughout his career he commanded three naval air stations, a seaplane tender and the aircraft carriers *Langley* and *Lexington*, as well as serving as Chief of Staff to

Commander Aircraft, Battle Force, and attending the Naval War College. Earlier in his career he had also commanded destroyers and been involved with aspects of gunnery. He began the war as commander of the *Saratoga* group and carried out raids around New Guinea. Fitch was in command of the *Lexington* group during the Battle of the Coral Sea. Later in the War he became Deputy Chief of Naval Operations for Air.

Adm. Kinkaid served as Fleet Gunnery Officer and Aide to the Commander-in-Chief, U.S. Fleet. He also spent some time as Secretary of the Navy's General Board and as a Naval Advisor at the 1931–32 Geneva Disarmament Conference, giving him valuable insight into the political implications of naval might. Kinkaid took command of USS *Indianapolis* in 1937. Service as Naval Attaché in Italy and Yugoslavia followed in 1938–41. In the months prior to U.S. entry into World War II, he commanded a destroyer squadron before becoming a rear admiral in 1942 when he gained command of a Pacific Fleet cruiser division. During the last half of the year, he commanded a task force built around the aircraft carrier *Enterprise*, participating in the long and difficult fight to seize and hold the southern Solomon Islands.

Herbert Leary, in charge of the Southwest Pacific Group, was a vice admiral at the time of the Battle of the Coral Sea. He had been in command of the *Lexington* task force since February 1942, which was the group that attacked the Japanese air base at Rabaul. He was put under the command of MacArthur on his arrival in Australia to head up the naval forces then in that area, and by May 1942 he was the overall commander of Task Force 44 (Rr. Adm. John C. Crace actually commanded the unit), the destroyers under Macinerny and all the salvage and air groups assigned to the theatre. This included the Task Group TG 17.9, which was basically a seaplane reconnaissance unit.

The American force was divided up into two main Task Forces, which were loose associations of ships pulled together to perform a certain function. The first Task Force was made up of an aircraft carrier group (Rr. Adm. Fitch), a support group (Rr. Adm. T. C. Kincaid and W. W. Smith), a destroyer division (the First under Capt. Early), a carrier escort group and a logistics group (Capt. Phillips). All of these were under the command of Fletcher with Rr. Adm. Fitch.

The second Task Force was under the command of Vice Adm. Herbert F. Leary and included Task Force 44 (Rr. Adm. J. C. Crace RN), a destroyer group (Cmdr. MacInerney), a salvage group and an air reconnaissance task group (Cmdr. de Baun). Also detailed to be involved was a submarine group (Capt. Christie).

Top: General Douglas Macarthur seen in August 1942.

Above: Rr Adm. Aubrey W. Fitch.

Above Left: Admiral C.W. Nimitz.

Left: Vice Adm. Frank Jack Fletcher.

The Imperial Japanese Navy

The commander of the Japanese Combined Fleet was Admiral Isoroku Yamamoto, who was the great thinker of the Japanese navy and the architect of the Midway plan. His key defining attribute in many people's eyes was that he had a cosmopolitan and highly sophisticated personality. He had worked and studied in the United States and had a far better idea than most other military commanders of the capabilities of the United States.

The main commander of Japanese forces in the area was Vice Adm. Shigeyoshi Inoue Commander-in-Chief of the 4th Imperial Fleet. Vice Adm. Shigeyoshi Inoue was a brilliant farsighted naval officer whose views on air power were a long way ahead of their time. As a naval strategist he had been head of the Naval Affairs Bureau of the Navy Ministry. As with many senior Japanese naval officers he had studied in Switzerland and France just after World War I. He became a rear admiral in 1936 and Chief of Naval Aviation in 1940. The inability of the Japanese Navy to occupy Port Moresby during Operation MO was largely seen as his responsibility and he was forced to return to Japan after the battle to lead a life of relative obscurity as commander of the naval college. During this battle Inoue was based at Rabaul and his headquarters were on board the cruiser *Kashima*.

Rr. Adm. Takeo Takagi graduated from the Naval Academy in 1912 and was something of an all-rounder, having served both as a staff officer on surface vessels and as an expert in torpedo warfare. He commanded the

strike force during the Battle of the Coral Sea and became the commander of the Sixth Submarine Fleet in 1943. He was killed on Saipan in 1944.

Rr. Adm. Aritomo Goto was the commander of the 6th Cruiser Squadron during the battle; he had commanded this unit from the beginning of the war. He fought at all the major actions in Rabaul and the Solomons but did not long survive the Coral Sea, being killed at Cape Esperance in 1942.

Rr. Adm. Chuichi Hara was commander of the 5th Carrier Division, which included the carriers *Shokaku* and *Zuikaku*. He missed the Battle of Midway because of the involvement of his force in the Coral Sea. In 1944 he became commander of the Fourth Fleet and survived till the end of the war. Hara's position during the battle reveals one of the peculiarities of Japanese command style, the adherence to strict rules of seniority. Hara would have been a wise choice for command of the entire Mobile Force, but Takagi got the post on the basis of seniority. Hara was to have exclusive command of the air operations in an irregular arrangement probably reflecting Takagi's lack of experience as an air commander.

In a book such as this it is common to deal with the high ranking commanders and their influence on events. But at the lower levels there are many commendable individuals, especially those who led the various air groups, without whom things could have gone very badly wrong. Commanding an air unit takes a special kind of control and awareness. On the American side officers such as Cmdr. W. B. Ault on the *Lexington* had to control the movements of all their air assets, he was killed during the battle. On the Japanese side the *Shokaku*'s Lt. Cmdr. Takahashi was a highly experienced and capable individual who orchestrated the attacks on the *Lexington* and the *Yorktown*.

Above Left: A 1945 view of Vice Adm. Thomas C. Kincaid aboard his flagship, USS *Wasatch*.

Left: A 1945 view of Vice Adm. Frederick C. Sherman aboard USS *Wasp*.

Above Right and Right: Fleet Adm. Isoroku Yamamoto, C-in-C of the Imperial Japanese Navy's Combined Fleet until his death. He was shot down by P-38 Lightnings over Bougainville on April 18, 1943, following the interception of a radio signal giving details of his location. His death was a great blow to Japanese morale.

OPPOSITE, ABOVE LEFT: Lt. (jg) Robert M. Elder, who won the Navy Cross.

OPPOSITE, ABOVE RIGHT: Another Navy Cross winner—Lt. Cdr. Dewitt S. Shumway.

OPPOSITE, BELOW: Adm. Elliot Buckmaster at the launching of the new USS *Yorktown*, January 21, 1943.

LEFT: Fleet Adm. Chester W. Nimitz (Right), Adm. Sir Bruce Fraser RN, and Adm. Raymond A. Spruance (Left) at a lunch on December 17, 1944.

BELOW: Captured Japanese newsreel possibly showing Adm. Goto watching his aircraft take-off. Note the "scoreboard" at left.

The opposing forces

Surface ships

Aircraft carriers

The two great Japanese carriers, *Zuikaku* and *Shokaku*, that made up the 5th Aircraft Carrier Division were the main striking forces of the Japanese Navy during the battle.

They were medium sized carriers with a displacement of 25,675 tons and a maximum speed of 34 knots. Both Japanese aircraft carriers were started in 1937 and *Shokaku* was completed on August 8, 1941, at Yokosuka Navy Yard. The *Zuikaku* was completed on August 25, 1941. Their dimensions were as follows:

	Shokaku	*Zuikaku*
Displacement	29,800 tons	25,675 tons
Length	820ft	844ft
Beam	85ft	85ft
Armament (both)	16 x 127mm (5in.) 40-cal. DP M1660, 42 x 25mm AA guns	

The aircraft compliment of the carriers was as follows: 16 Zero fighters, including four spare machines, 18 Type 99 bombers, including six spares, and 18 Type 97 bombers, including six spares. Slightly later the complement was increased to 18 fighters and 27 of each type of bomber.

The *Shoho* was much lighter escort vessel, she was built at Yokosuka yard and, as with many carriers of the period, was a conversion of an earlier ship, the *Takasaki*.

	Weight	Length	Beam	Armament
Shoho	11,262 tons	660ft	59ft	8 x 127mm
	(5in.) 40-cal. DP M1660, 8 x 25mm AA guns			

On the American side the two major carriers were the USS *Lexington* and the *Yorktown*. The *Lexington* was finished on October 3, 1925, by the Fore River ship building company. She had a displacement of 33,000 tons was crewed by a complement of 2,122 sailors. She was originally intended as a battlecruiser, but following World War I was converted to an aircraft carrier. It was possible to carry 90 aircraft aboard but this seldom happened in practice and routinely carried just 71 in four squadrons: 36 Douglas Dauntless SBD.2-3 dive-bombers in two squadrons, 12 Douglas TBD Devastator torpedo bombers and 23 Grumman F4F.3 Wildcats.

	Lexington	*Yorktown*
Displacement	33,000 tons	19,900 tons
Length	830ft	761ft
Beam	105.5ft	83.25ft
Armament (both)	8 x 8in. 55-cal.,	8 x 5in. 38-cal.,
	12 x 5in. AA	16 x 1.1in. AA
	4 x 6-pdr saluting	16 x .50-cal. MGs
	8 x 50-cal. MGs	

ABOVE: Japanese Yubari-class light cruiser.

ABOVE RIGHT: Japanese carrier *Shokaku*—one of the casualties of the battle.

OPPOSING FORCES

Naval forces and air force available at the Battle of the Coral Sea

JAPANESE

5th Carrier Division (Hara)
Zuikaku
Shokaku
5th Cruiser Division
Myoko
Haguro
Destroyers
Ariake
Yugure
Shiratsuyu
Ushio
Akebono
Tanker
Toho Maru

Landing Forces
Tulagi Group (Shima)
Minelayer
Okinishima
Seaplane tender
Kawa Maru
22nd Destroyer Division
Kikuzuki
Yuzuki
Transports
Asuman Maru
Tama Maru
Two minesweepers plus auxiliary vessels.

MO group (Kajioka)
Cruisers
Yubari
Destroyers
Oite
Asanagi
Uzuki
Mutsuki
Yunagi
Yahoi

18th Cruiser Division (Marushige)
Cruisers
Tenryu
Tatsuta
Seaplane transport
Kamikawa Maru
Gunboats
Keijo Maru
Seikai Maru
Nikkai Maru
Minelayer
Tsugaru

Covering Force (Goto)
Cruisers
Aoba
Kako
Kinugasa
Furutaka
Aircraft carrier
Shoho
Destroyer
Sazanami
Fuel Tanker
Hiro Maru
Submarines
Two RO class
Five I class

Aircraft resources
Shokaku Air Group
18 A6M.2 Zero fighters
27 Aichi D3A Val dive-bombers
27 Nakajima 97 B5N Kate torpedo carriers
Zuikaku Air Group
18 A6M.2 Zero fighters
27 Aichi D3A Val dive-bombers
27 Nakajima 97 B5N Kate torpedo carriers
Shoho Air Group
16 A6M.2 Zero fighters
19 Nakajima 97 B5N Kate torpedo carriers
25th Air Group
44 A6M.2 Zero fighters
41 Mitsubishi Nell bombers
13 Kawanishi HK6 reconnaissance flying boats
Lae
16 A6M.2 Zero fighters
Buna
7 Mitsubishi Nell bombers
Shortland
3 Kawanishi HK6 reconnaissance flying boats
4 light seaplanes
Tulagi
6 A6M.2 Zero fighters
Truk
44 A6M.2 Zero fighters
41 Mitsubishi Nell bombers
Deboyne
12 light reconnaissance seaplanes

UNITED STATES FORCES
Task Force 17
Task Group 17.2 (Attack Group)
Heavy cruisers
Minneapolis
New Orleans
Astoria
Chester
Portland
Destroyer screen
Phelps
Dewey
Farragut
Aylwin
Monaghan

Task Force 44 (TF 17.3)
Heavy cruisers
Australia
Chicago
Light cruisers
Hobart
Destroyer screen
Perkins
Walke
Farragut

Task Group 17.5 (Carrier Group)
Aircraft carriers
Yorktown (CV-5)
Lexington (CV-2)
Destroyer screen
Morris
Anderson
Hammann
Russell

Task Group 17.6 (Fueling Group)
Oilers
Neosho
Tippecanoe
Destroyers
Sims
Worden

Task Group 17.9 (Search Group)
Seaplane tanker
Tangier
Submarine patrol group
Seven patrolling submarines
Aircraft resources
VP71 – 6 Catalina PBY flying boats
VP73 – 6 Catalina PBY flying boats

Yorktown air group
VF42 – 21 Grumman F4F Wildcat fighters
VB5 – 19 Douglas Dauntless SBD.2/3 dive-bombers (bombing role)
VS5 – 19 Douglas Dauntless SBD.2/3 dive-bombers (scouting role)
VT5 – 13 Douglas TBD.1 Devastators torpedo carriers
Lexington air group
VF2 – 23 Grumman F4F Wildcat fighters
VB2 – 18 Douglas Dauntless SBD.2/3 dive-bombers (bombing role)
VS2 – 18 Douglas Dauntless SBD.2/3 dive-bombers (scouting role)
VT2 – 12 Douglas TBD.1 Devastators torpedo carriers

Cruisers

There were both American and Australian heavy cruisers present at the Battle of the Coral Sea. The concept of the cruiser in the U.S. Navy was as a larger version of the destroyer, though there were differences notably in the size of main armament and armor protection. In American service these vessels ranged from 8,000–18,000 tons and had between six and ten 8in. guns as well as secondary AA armament. Light cruisers were armed with 6-in. rather than 8-in. primary armament with a secondary armament often equal to the heavies. One of the principal differences between the Japanese and American cruisers at this stage in the war was that the Japanese retained torpedoes on their heavy cruisers as standard. The U.S. heavy cruisers were mainly of the Minneapolis, Portland and Northampton classes their details were as follows:

ABOVE: A 1937 view of CV-5 *Yorktown*.

LEFT: CV-2 *Lexington*— **another prewar photograph, this one dated 1933.**

	Displacement	Length	Beam	Armor	Armament
Minneapolis class	9,950 tons	588ft	61.75ft	5in. side, 3in. turret	9 x 8in., 8 x 5 in. AA, 2 x 3-pdr, 10 x MGs
Portland class	9,800 tons	584ft	66ft	3–4in. side, 3in. turret	9 x 8in., 8 x 5in. AA, 2 x 3-pdr, 10 x MGs
Northampton class	9,050 tons	570ft	66	3in. side, 1.5in. turret	9 x 8in., 8 x 5 in. AA, 2 x 3-pdr, 8 x MGs

The Australian cruisers present at the battle were the *Australia* and the *Hobart*:

	Displacement	Length	Beam	Armor	Armament
Australia	10,000 tons	630ft	68.5	4in. deck, 2in. turret	8 x 8in., 8 x 4in. AA, 4 x 3-pdr, 4 x 2-pdr pom poms, 4 x MGs, 8 x Lewis guns.
Hobart	6,980 tons	555ft	56.25ft	3in. side, 1in. turret	8 x 6in., 8 x 4in. AA, 4 X 4-pdr, 10 x MGs.

RIGHT: The flightdeck of this U.S. carrier is a hive of activity as a Douglas SBD comes in to land.

BELOW: USS *Marblehead*, CL-2. This ship was attacked by Japanese aircraft in 1942 and severly damaged.

OPPOSITE, TOP: IJN carrier *Zuikaku* seen in 1944 with a Grumman TBF Avenger overhead. The TBF entered service in spring 1942 and first saw action at Midway. The *Zuikaku* and her sister *Shokaku* were the first Japanese carriers planned after the naval limitation treaties of the postwar period lapsed. *Zuikaku* was sunk at Luzon on October 25, 1944.

OPPOSITE, CENTER: IJN destroyer *Ushio* in Yokosuka Habor, September 13, 1945.

OPPOSITE, BELOW: A Japanese minesweeper.

ABOVE: The cruiser USS *Chester* seen in 1930.

RIGHT: The cruiser USS *Minneapolis* seen in 1934.

OPPOSITE, ABOVE: The Japanese cruiser *Myoko*.

OPPOSITE, BELOW: The Japanese cruiser *Haguro* seen in 1936.

Japanese cruisers such as the *Aoba* were really 1920s designs. At 7,100 tons she could manage a speed of 33 knots maximum. Her armament was 6 x 8in. guns in three twin turrets, 4 x 4.7in. anti-aircraft guns, 10 x machine guns and 12 x 21in. torpedo tubes. The armored decks and belt were 2in. thick. In contrast the *Myoko*, Admiral Takagi's flagship, was much more heavily armored and gunned. Her main armament was 10 x 8in. 50-cal. guns in five twin turrets. She also had six 4.7in. AA guns and 8 x 47mm AA guns, plus 8 x machine guns and 8 x torpedo tubes. She had a much more substantial belt of 3in. and a 2–3in. armored deck. The other Japanese cruisers fell into Myoko, Kako and Yubari Classes:

	Displacement	Length	Beam	Armor	Armament
Myoko class	10,000 tons	630ft	62.5ft	3in. side, 3in. turret	10 x 8in., 6 x 4.7in. AA, 8 x 47mm AA, 8 x MGs
Kako class	7,100 tons	595ft	50.75ft	2in. side, 1.5in. turret	6 x 8in., 4 x 4.7in. AA, 10 x MGs
Yubari class	2,890 tons	435ft	39.5ft	2in. side	6 x 5.5in., 1 x 3in. AA, 2 x MGs

Destroyers

The workhorse of both navies during this battle was the destroyer, without which no large capital ship could be defended. A typical example of this was the *Anderson* of Task Force 17. She was one of the Sims-class that had been part of the pre-war destroyer program. At 1,570 tons she was armed with 5 x 5in. guns, four torpedo tubes and depth charge racks. These ships were inclined to be top heavy but their use in aircraft defense was to be critical. American destroyers of the Farragut, Sims, Porter and Mahan classes were all present at the battle and their comparative characteristics were as follows:

Class	Sims	Farragut	Porter	Mahan
Displacement (tons)	1,570	1,395	1,850	1,500
Length	341ft	341.25ft	381ft	341.25ft
Beam	35ft	34ft	37ft	34.75ft
Armament	Sims—5 x 5in. 4 x MGs, 12 x 2in. TTs			
	Farragut—5 x 5in., 4 x MGs, 8 x 21in. TTs			
	Porter—8 x 5 in. 38-cal., 8 x 1-pdr, 2 x MGs, 8 x 21in. TTs			
	Mahan—5 x 5in. 4 x MGs, 12 x 2in. TTs			

The destroyers could reach speeds of between 36 and 37 knots, whereas the maximum speed of a carrier such as the *Shoho* was only 28 knots.

The Japanese destroyers of the Hatuharu class and the Hubuki class had the following characteristics:

	Displacement	Length	Beam	Armament
Hatuharu class	1,368 tons	337.75ft	32.5ft	5 x 5in.,
2 machine guns, 6 x 21in. TT				
Hubuki class	1,700 tons	371.5ft	33.75ft	6 x 5in.,
4 AA machine guns, 9 x 21in. TTs				
Both classes were capable of a maximum speed of 34 knots.				

Left: Two-man Japanese submarine that grounded near Bellows Field on December 7, 1941, and was later brought to Pearl Harbor. Another was rammed and sunk in Pearl.

Far Left: The destroyer USS *Farragut* seen prewar in 1934.

All of these specifications are drawn from sources written in 1941 and as such do not take into account the upgrades that many vessels underwent between the end of 1941 and 1942. The *Lexington* in particular was upgunned with many smaller caliber anti-aircraft weapons, as were many Japanese ships.

Submarines

Some mention of submarines must be made here even though they played no direct role in the battle. There were submarine groups attached to the naval forces of both sides. The Japanese had seven allocated to Operation MO of which five were I class and two were RO class. They were known as the patrol group and raiding group respectively. Submarines were excellent reconnaissance vessels and they could be used in all sorts of different roles. As lookouts they could cover a known area of the sea undetected whilst reporting back enemy sightings. The Americans had a submarine group of seven vessels patrolling the southeastern approaches to Australia.

Anti-aircraft guns

Probably the most interesting aspect of the Battle of the Coral Sea was the fact that it was air power and air power alone that decided the issue. The large main gun armament of each ship was of secondary importance to the air defense weapons. This has often been overlooked during this battle so it is my intention to analyze the differences in the anti-aircraft defenses of the two fleets.

It was clear that, from the point of view of aircraft defense, the fleet that could put up the most accurate, effective anti-aircraft barrage would be the one that would be best defended. This needed a combination of good morale and training for the gunners, accurate fire direction equipment and the right type of weapon. Traditionally the anti-aircraft defense of a ship was divided between the long-range high-altitude guns, such as the 5in. 38-cal. so favored by the Americans, and the low-level short-range guns such as the 20mm Oerlikon.

The American 5in. 38-cal. gun was the commonest weapon for primary air defense. There were three main mountings for it: the pedestal mount, the base ring and the dual-purpose (DP) twin. This weapon was designed to counter bombers attacking on the level at distance. These aircraft needed a long run to their target and if they were engaged at long range their attack runs would be upset.

Left: The Japanese 1st Destroyer Squadron on maneuvers in 1939.

Right: A U.S. Navy 5in. 38-cal. gun.

The days of the proximity fuse were in the future and long time delay fuses were used with this sort of weapon. From the gunnery report of the *Lexington* it is clear that time-fused shells were preset:

> Subsequently, certain of the 5in. group control offi-
> cers attempted to designate fuse settings to be used
> [the 5in. ammunition was all pre-set to either 5.2
> seconds, 3 seconds, or 2.2 seconds]. It is consid-
> ered that they erred in so doing. The surviving 5in.
> were used against torpedo planes. They were not
> mobile enough against the shallow glides and dis-
> persed bearing of the dive-bombers.
> (*Naval Intelligence Combat Reports*)

In the 1930s the dive-bomber was perceived as the main aerial threat and that is how it turned out to be. A high-angle, automatic weapon was thought to be the counter. Both the Americans and the British used the Bofors gun, which was a Swedish design made under license. During the Battle of the Coral Sea none of the Allied ships were armed with it. Although both the Japanese and Americans favored a 5in. heavy anti-aircraft gun they used very different sorts of light anti-aircraft weapon. Initially the US favored the Browning .50-cal. machine gun and the homegrown 1.1in. heavy machine gun for their anti-aircraft defense at close range, but they soon realized that these guns, particularly the latter, were unreliable and compli-cated to use. Therefore, by 1940 it had been decided to install the Bofors and the Swiss-designed Oerlikon 20mm anti-aircraft guns. Any photographs of American vessels in the Pacific after 1942 shows them bristling with these weapons. In fact Oerlikons were beginning to be installed at the start of 1941. The Oerlikon needed no power supply and could be bolted to the deck almost anywhere on a ship. It had a spring recuperator, could easily be repaired and had a high rate of fire. However, the smaller 20mm projectile did not have the destructive capacity of the 40mm round. From July 1942 onwards, American ships were armed with the larger 40mm weapon.

The gunnery report on the *Lexington* quotes the fol-lowing armament: 5in. guns, 1.1in. machine guns, 20mm Oerlikons and .5in. Browning stacks. The crews operating these guns seem to have been in control and alert through-out the battle, in fact the gunnery officer O'Donnell stated of his men:

> The fire discipline and distribution of the automatic
> weapons was splendid. No enemy plane was seen to

attack without being fired upon. The accuracy of the fire was fairly good, as nearly as could be judged.

The air defense of the Japanese fleet relied on a wide range of weaponry. Probably the most popular weapon was the Type 89 40-cal. 12.7cm gun, though other 4.7in. and 3.9in. weapons were used. Part of the reason for this was that the Japanese, like most other countries, were using older designs as well as those that were specifically designed to be fired at a high angle for anti-aircraft defense. The Type 89 was one of the few weapons that was specifically designed for the purpose and its main target was the dive-bomber. Although larger caliber guns could engage the slower moving and horizontally attacking torpedo bombers, dive-bombers posed the greatest threat to the fleet. The Type 89 could fire 14 rounds per minute at 90 degrees elevation. Two other larger caliber weapons were developed during 1937 and 1938, and these were the Type 98 10cm (65-cal.) and the 8cm (60-cal) high angle weapons.

The gun itself was only one part of a system that had to make sure that a shell arrived at the right time near a fast-moving and erratic target. This form of prediction required a complicated fire control system that could calculate the speed and direction of an aircraft compared that to that of the ship and then order the right guns to fire at the target. It is not the intention of this book to go into the

LEFT: A pair of 40mm AA guns in a single mounting. This weapon became the principal close-range AA defense weapon on U.S. ships after 1942.

OPPOSITE, ABOVE LEFT: 5in. AA guns on USS *Enterprise* firing at a target drone during a simulated torpedo attack, March 1942.

OPPOSITE, ABOVE RIGHT: Marines standing by the 20mm guns on USS *Yorktown*.

OPPOSITE, BELOW: Guncrew of a 1.1in. AA gun on USS *Enterprise* preparing to fire, April 1942.

BELOW: Testing a 20mm. AA gun on USS *Jouett*, 1942.

complexities of fire control, it is sufficient to say that what were needed for the guns to fire accurately were an elevation angle, a training angle and a fuse time for the guns. By the time of the Battle of the Coral Sea the Type 94 HA angle fire direction equipment was being used on Japanese vessels. It consisted of a rangefinder and director on the superstructure of the ship and a calculating computer deep in the bowels of the vessel, as was the case with Allied vessels. This area was known in Allied parlance as the transmission station and was one of the most vital parts of the ship, which explains its location in a protected metal box. There was an earlier version known as the Type 91, this was not as satisfactory but was also in use during the battle.

Japanese light anti-aircraft weapons were based on Hotchkiss designs and, as ever, the Japanese had studied the design and development of foreign weapon systems in minute detail. They relied on the heavy 25mm gun as an equivalent to the American Oerlikon and a 8mm gun for close-range defense. In 1935 the Japanese decided to

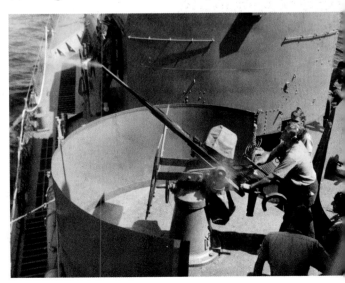

200lb bomb load. Although the Wildcat was in many ways inferior to the Japanese Zero its inherent survivability, coupled with the innovative defensive tactics used by U.S. pilots, ensured that it held its own in aerial combat. One such tactic was known as the Thatch Weave, as Lt. James Thatch developed it. The formation required a gap of about 550–750yds abreast between friendly aircraft. If an enemy aircraft latched on to either aircraft, both pilots turned towards each other. This resulted in the wingmans's guns coming to bear on the aircraft pursuing the primary aircraft. Repeating this maneuver forced the pursuing enemy aircraft to either break off the pursuit or face multiple head-on attacks from the wingman.

Against the Wildcat stood the Japanese A6M Zero fighter. This exceptional aircraft had been built to a design concept that sacrificed everything for speed and maneuverability. The designers, Mitsubishi, had created an aircraft that caused the Americans severe problems in combat. The Zero had a similar maximum speed as the F4F but its climb rate was greater and it was much lighter. The Model 21 was armed with two 20mm cannon and two 7.7mm machine guns. It could also carry a 250lb bomb. The one great drawback to the Zero was its lack of both armor protection and a self-sealing fuel tank. This combination led to it being extremely combustible when hit.

replace their British made 2-pdrs because of their slow rate of fire, unreliable nature and difficulties of construction. A design based upon the French Hotchkiss machine gun was selected as the replacement. Japanese modifications included the replacement of some parts by castings and the use of German Rheinmetall-type flash suppressors. The 25mm Type 96 was widely used throughout the Japanese Navy, with about 33,000 guns being produced. It had an effective rate of fire of 110-120 rpm and there were single, double and triple mountings. There are few real accounts of its defensive use during the Battle of the Coral Sea but the Japanese considered this gun to be an excellent weapon. The magazines for the Type 96 held only 15 rounds, so frequent stoppages for changes of magazine were required. The Japanese were the only major navy of World War II not to develop close-range anti-aircraft machine guns larger than 25mm (1in.).

A 13.7mm machine gun was widely used on Japanese ships throughout World War II. Its design was again based upon a French Hotchkiss machine gun and it was similar in design to the 25mm gun, though its magazine held 30 rounds.

Aircraft

Fighters

The main U.S. fighter used at the Battle of the Coral Sea was the Grumman F4F Wildcat, which had been in service since 1940 having replaced the previous series of biplanes. As a fighter it was robust and could be used to devastating effect in the right hands. Its Wright R1830-76 engine enabled it to fly at a maximum speed of 330mph, though its climb rate was poor compared to the Japanese Zero. It had four .50-cal. machine guns and could carry a

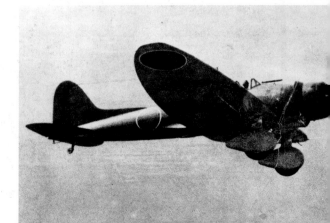

Comparative performance:					
	Power	Max. speed	Climb speed	Range	Armament
Grumman F4F Wildcat	1,200HP	329mph	2,000ft per minute	844 miles	4 x .50-cal. MGs and a 200lb bomb load
Mitsubishi A6M2 Zero	940HP	331mph	2,571ft per minute	1,470 miles	2 x 20mm cannon, 2 x 7.7mm MGs and a 250lb bomb load

Dive-bombers

The Americans had a very reliable accurate dive-bomber in the Douglas SBD Dauntless. Stability, a vital attribute for dive-bombers, was a prominent feature of the Dauntless's flying characteristics and ensured that it stayed in the American arsenal for longer than many other aircraft. It carried a bomb load of one 900lb bomb and two 90lb bombs, and was armed with two forward firing machine guns and two flexible machine guns. This was a substantial range of armament for a bomber and the Dauntless was used as a fighter on several occasions. The main drawback of the Dauntless was that it was very slow in horizontal flight. There was also a problem when the aircraft dived from high to low altitude. According to Barret Tillman:

The SBD.1-4 was armed with a three power telescopic sight, a holdover from the open cockpit aircraft of the 1930s. The pilot looked through the tube, lining up the crosshairs on the target while keeping a ball much like that of a turn and bank indicator centered in its groove. The centered ball told him the aircraft was level in the dive, otherwise the bomb would go off on a tangent when released.However, the sight was prone to condensation and could fog up at this critical moment.

In organizational terms, the 1942 dive-bomber squadrons usually consisted of 18 aircraft flying in three divisions of two three-plane sections. Each section flew in an inverted V formation. Weather often affected the way in which the unit could work but visual contact could be made at 30–40 miles from the target in clear weather at 18,000ft. When the dive-bomber went in for an attack he went to what was called pushover, which is the point at which the plane started its dive. Pushover altitude was at about 15,000 feet and the aircraft were normally spaced

LEFT: The Mitsubishi A6M Zero-Sen, codenamed "Zeke" by the Allies, was the best-known of Japan's fighters. Over 10,000 were built and it was used as a carrier- or land-based fighter, fighter-bomber, dive-bomber, and, latterly, as a suicide bomber.

OPPOSITE, TOP: U.S. Navy .50-cal. machine gun mounting.

OPPOSITE, CENTER: October 1942 shot of a Zero in U.S. colors being evaluated above San Diego.

OPPOSITE, BELOW: Aichi D3A1 Navy Type 99 carrier bomber. The mainstay of the Japanese naval airforce in 1942.

1,500 feet apart; one diving after the other. On its descent the dive speed was about 276mph. This was controlled by the dive brakes easily recognizable on a Dauntless as the flaps with holes in them. When the Dauntless was being chased by a Japanese fighter using the dive brakes was one way of making the attacker overshoot. The bomb was usually released at about 1,500–2,000ft above the target.

The Dauntless acted as a scout as well as a bomber and a carrier group carried four squadrons of the scout and bomber variants.

The Japanese had not been slow in appreciating the value of the dive-bomber on land or at sea and when they produced their first monoplane dive-bomber, the Aichi 99 Val, it proved to be a formidable weapon, at least for early part of the war. It had a fixed undercarriage and a crew of three men. It is believed that the Japanese had based some of the features of the Aichi Val on those of the Ju 87 Stuka and on the basis of their experiments produced an all-metal aircraft. The Val had a maximum speed of 267mph and a range of 930 miles. It was said to be extremely accurate and very stable as a dive-bomber. It remained an important weapon in the Japanese armory throughout the war.

Comparative performance:

	Power	Max.speed	Climb speed	Range	Armament
Douglas Dauntless SBD.3	1,000HP	246mph	9,000ft in 6 minutes	1,100 miles	2 x .50-cal. MGs, 2 x .30-cal. MGs, 1 x 900lb and 2 x 90lb bombs
Aichi 99 Val	1,300HP	267mph	9,000ft in 5 minutes	930 miles	2 x .30-cal. MGs, 1 x flexible .30-cal. MG, 1 x 500lb and 2 x 120lb, or 4 x 120lb bombs.

Torpedo bombers

At this stage in the war the main U.S. torpedo plane was the Douglas TBD Devastator, which came to the fore in 1935. By the time of the Pacific War it was an antiquated aircraft. it was slow in horizontal flight and easy to shoot down, as the early battles showed. The aircraft required three crew to operate it and very few of these aircraft scored a hit during the Battle of the Coral Sea.

The main Japanese torpedo plane was the Nakajima 97 Kate. This was the first fully Japanese designed torpedo plane and it had a crew of three. It was designed so that it could carry out horizontal bombing and low level torpedo attacks. Most of the torpedo bombers that entered the war for the combatant nations were obsolete before they actually carried out any attacks, the British Swordfish and the Devastator in particular, but the Kate was state of the art in 1939. It could carry a torpedo weighing 1,600lb and had a maximum speed of 235mph and a cruising speed of 163mph, which compared favorably to the 128mph that the Devastator could muster.

Comparative performance:

	Power	Max.speed	Climb speed	Range	Armament
Nakajima 97 Kate	1,000HP	235mph	9,000ft in 7 minutes	634 miles	1 x .30-cal.
moveable machine gun, 1 Type 96 torpedo or a bomb load up to 1000lb					
Douglas TBD Devastator	900HP	205mph	700ft per minute		1 x .30-cal.
machine gun fixed, 1 x .30-cal. machine gun flexible, 1 Mark 13 torpedo					

Torpedoes and bombs

Two weapons stand out as being particularly effective against ships during the Battle of the Coral Sea: the aerial bomb and the torpedo. The latter, along with the mine, was responsible for the greatest number of ship losses of World War II and was understandably feared by surface commanders. When it was delivered by air its extended range dramatically increased its potency.

In the United States pre-war torpedo designs were almost exclusively dominated by the company E. W. Bliss and Co. (known as Bliss-Leavitt) whose weapons were still in use at the beginning of the war. The Mk 9 was the last torpedo manufactured by them whilst the Mk 10 was the

ABOVE: Douglas TBD Devastator launching a Mk 13 torpedo in a prewar trial.

LEFT AND ABOVE LEFT: Douglas SBD Dauntlesses on the deck of USS *Enterprise*, May 1942. Note the early-war identification stars.

last designed by them. Bliss and the Navy were at loggerheads in the early part of the century over the intention of the company to sell their ideas abroad and from 1907 the U.S. Navy began to develop its own production and testing facility known as the NTS or Naval Torpedo Station. Mks 11 and 12 were pure NTS products, but altogether only a few hundred were built. It was the Mk 13

American torpedoes of WWII				
	Mark 11	Mark 13	Mark 14	Mark 15
Weight	3,512lb	2,216lb	3,280lb	3,840lb
Length	22.6ft	14.24ft	20.5ft	24ft
Speed	27knts	33.5knts	46knts	33.5knts
Range	15,000yds	6,300yds	4,500yds	10,000yds
Warhead	500lb	578lb	644lb	825lb

torpedo that was to be used by the Americans as the main armament for their aircraft. It was 14.24ft in length and had a diameter of 22.5in. Its maximum speed was 33.5 knots, slow compared to other submarine-launched weapons. The Mk 13 structure was designed to survive being launched at a speed of 100 knots and from a height of 50ft. Accessories were required to maintain satisfactory aerodynamics and prevent damage on entry into the water.

In Japan the aerial torpedo had reached a high state of technical development. The Japanese had opted for a pure oxygen system of propulsion, which made their torpedoes perform far more spectacularly than those of the Americans. There were several models in use at the time of the Battle of the Coral Sea, Types 91 to 96. These torpedoes were very similar in range and weight and the Type 91 Mod 2 had a length of 17.7ft, weighed 1,841lb and could travel at 41 knots. It was first deployed in April 1941,

and carried by the Kate torpedo bombers that attacked Pearl Harbor. This torpedo was far faster than that employed by the Americans and therefore much harder to maneuver away from. In addition to this the Japanese had developed other mechanisms to protect the torpedo when dropped into the water from height. American commentators said that they could see wooden boxes protecting the head and tail of the torpedoes when they were being attacked.

In contrast to the complexity of the torpedo a bomb is a simple device. Normally it is a steel shell filled with high explosive, sometimes with a base fuse and sometimes with a nose fuse. Even with a small explosive charge an aerial-delivered bomb can be a devastating weapon. Many were designed to pierce armor and, with a delayed action fuse, they could penetrate into the bowels of a ship before exploding. Bombs were often converted naval munitions and when attacking ships the preferred weight during this battle was about 1,000lb on both sides. The Aichi Val dive-bomber could carry one 500lb bomb under its fuselage plus (D3A1) two 120lb bombs, or (D3A2) four 120lb bombs under its wings. The Douglas SBD Dauntless could carry one 1,000lb or 500lb bomb under the fuselage or two 250lb or 100lb. bombs under its wings.

Japanese torpedoes of WWII				
	Type 93 Mod 1	Type 93 Mod 3	Type 95 Mod1	Type 96
Weight	5,952lb	6,173lb	3,671lb	3,671lb
Length	30ft	30ft	23ft	23ft
Speed	36knts	36knts	45knts	48knts
Range	40,000yds	30,000yds	12,000yds	4500yds
Warhead	1,080lb	1,720lb	1,091lb	1,091lb

Morale and fighting experience

It should be remembered that the crews of the two U.S. carriers were at a state of very high morale during this battle. There is a good reason for this; the *Lexington* had taken part in reprisal raids against the Japanese in the central Pacific. These were isolated successes set against the backdrop of the series of defeats suffered by the British, Americans and Dutch in early 1942. The "Lady Lex," as she was known, was a relatively new ship and her captain Frederick C Sherman was very popular with the crew. The one drawback of the crew was their inexperience and this would show during the battle. The *Yorktown* under Capt. Buckmaster had also been part of the reprisal raids under Fletcher and had attacked islands in the Marshall chain, her crew too were said to be riding high on their newfound success.

The Japanese aviators had much more experience than their U.S. counterparts. As a good example of their activities the history of a fighter squadron assigned to the *Shokaku* shows how they performed. Originally assigned to Kyushu in October 1941, part of the unit was involved in the attack on Pearl Harbor. As part of the 5th Carrier Division they took part in attacks on Rabaul and Lae on January 8, 1942. In March 1942 they were in the Indian Ocean and they raided Trincomalee before their involvement in the Battle of the Coral Sea. Similarly, the fighter groups of the *Zuikaku* were continuously involved in action from the Pearl Harbor until the beginnings of the Coral Sea. The experience gained by these operations undoubtedly gave the Japanese an advantage.

ABOVE: Japanese torpedo-bombers were better than those of the U.S. Navy at the start of the war, the Kate being a much better aircraft than the Devastator.

LEFT: Torpedo bombers on the deck of USS *Enterprise*.

BELOW: Only some 129 Douglas TBD Devastators were built and losses were heavy due to poor defensive armament, but it could carry a 21in. torpedo or 1,000lb bomb and inflicted heavy damage on Japanese forces at the start of the Pacific war. This one is about to land on USS *Enterprise* in May 1942.

Logistics

It is an often-ignored fact that the supply and maintenance of vessels at sea is as important to the success of an action as the offensive capabilities of a fleet. Large vessels such as an aircraft carrier or battlecruiser are not endowed with huge fuel tanks and need to be re-supplied irregularly. Ammunition, food and other essentials can only be stored on board up to a point. Therefore any task force had to have a supply train in tow. Before 1943 the U.S. Navy had a shortage of supply vessels and the later war organization was not fully in place. As an example of the amount of fuel used a carrier task force of three carriers, two heavy cruisers, light cruisers and destroyers would use 50 tons of fuel oil in one hour traveling at 12 knots. This meant that a tanker of say 9,600 tons capacity would need to refuel the ships every eight days. The *Lexington* used 4.9 tons an hour and had a fuel tank of 3,600 tons capacity. The *Shokaku* used 6.2 tons an hour and had a slightly larger tank at 4,100 tons. At the other end of the scale a Fletcher-class destroyer used 1.1 tons an hour with a tank capacity of 492 tons. If one takes into account the need to fuel aircraft a second supply problem becomes obvious: aircraft fuel also needed to be stored onboard. The *Shokaku*'s original compliment of 72 aircraft needed 187,000 gallons of aviation fuel, of which 2,600 gallons of fuel were allocated to each aircraft allowing roughly nine flights. The *Yorktown* carried 178,000 gallons allowing an average of 6 or 7 sorties per aircraft. It has also been estimated that the ammunition required for an Essex-class aircraft carrier was about 325 tons, including two torpedoes per bomber and 18 bombs per dive-bomber.

The complexities of supply and distribution were enormous. Food, ammunition, engine spares, and all the

RIGHT: DD-456 USS *Rodman* is refueled at sea. This image gives a good view of her 5in. guns.

other needs of the navy had to be carried with them. In an area such as the Coral Sea the local ports were frequently not big enough to deal with supplying large amounts of stores. Therefore both sides had to use a small number of ports and facilities for their operations. Rabaul was the base of operations for the Japanese and this in some ways counterbalanced the fact that their landing force under Rr. Adm. Koso Abe had a whole fleet of small supply ships attached to it. With an average speed of 12–15 knots these ships were sitting ducks for American naval aviators. Rabaul needed to be supplied from Japan and the distance was roughly 2,900 miles. At an average speed it took a merchant ship 48 days to arrive at the Solomon Islands from the nearest of the home islands. The threat of enemy submarines and bad weather fronts in the Pacific meant that commanders could not rely on a shipment from Japan arriving in one piece. The Japanese controlled most of the good ports in the Pacific area in 1942 and so the allies relied on being supplied from Australia or—more realistically—from Midway and

then the United States itself. Therefore large fleet trains were required to sail with the fleet and supply it. In the case of the battle of the Coral Sea the Logistics force consisted of the tankers *Neosho* and *Tippecanoe* protected by two destroyers. There was also a seaplane replenisher called the AV8 *Tangier* based at Nouméa on the island of New Caledonia.

As a final point about how the destruction of the supply train could affect the ability of naval vessels to wage war, we can look at what happened to the problems after the tanker *Neosho* was sunk. The damage sustained by the *Yorktown* during the battle meant that she leaked fuel and the need to retire from the battle area to carry out repairs and replenishment would be essential. There were only so many places that the Task Force could go: south and west to Australia or to Tongatabu, which is what Fletcher eventually did. Although the naval command had dispatched two oilers to Fletcher's group under Halsey there was serious risk that these vessels could well be sunk by Japanese aircraft or vessels on their way to rendezvous.

THIS PAGE AND OPPOSITE: Refueling at sea was of major importance to both sides during the Pacific war, albeit a risky business at times as these pictures of USS *Neosho* (AO-23) show. The photograph opposite shows *Neosho* refueling the *Yorktown* at sea on May 1, 1942, just before the battle. *Neosho* was one of the casualties of the battle, scuttled on May 11 after being crippled by bombs dropped from "Val" bombers from *Zuikaku* on May 7.

The battle arena

The Pacific Ocean is a vast area of water. We know much more about the geography and climate than was known in 1942 and so to commanders of both sides it was with some trepidation that they planned for the battle. Dominating the area are two large landmasses—New Guinea and Australia. The former is an island to the northeast of Australia that was, and still is, in many areas impenetrable. The Owen Stanley mountain ranges separate the two halves of the island, northern and southern, and it is completely covered in rain forest and jungle—hardly the kind of place to carry out a military campaign. The Japanese occupied Rabaul on New Britain and it was their inability to cross the Owen Stanley Mountains that forced them to sail to Port Moresby. The Coral Sea is an area southeast of Papua New Guinea and to the south of the Solomon Islands. On its eastern side New Caledonia encloses it. It is approximately 1,000 miles from Townsville on the eastern coast of Australia to the island of Santa Isabel in the Solomons and approximately 1,000 miles to New Caledonia to Samarai on the tip of New Guinea. These four points roughly enclose the Coral Sea in 1,000,000 square miles of ocean. It is effectively very close to the Australian mainland, hence its strategic significance. During the 19th century many ships were wrecked in the area due to constantly shifting sand cays, and the reefs and islands have often been named after the ships that foundered there.

All of the islands in the Solomons group are particularly tropical, crowned with dense jungle and some mountains. The Japanese decided to make their seaplane base at Tulagi, which lies to the north of Guadalcanal. Its sister island, Florida, is east of Tulagi but is very close to it. To the southwest of the Solomon Islands lie the Louisade Archipelago and the strategically important area known as the Jomard Passage. This was the area through which the Japanese had to pass to get to Port Moresby, their invasion objective. The weather is similar to the tropical maritime Tasman air mass, but it is warmer, coming from further north in the Coral Sea and tropical western Pacific Ocean. This air mass affects the Central and North Queensland coast most of the year, and can bring heavy rainfall if associated with tropical cyclones or tropical depressions. High humidity and frequent rains mean that It is a normally good source of moisture for eastern Australia generally and the eastern seaboard especially. The same types of weather pattern can create huge cloud formations and snap tropical storms. For a naval air force this changing climate could be a useful asset or a huge disadvantage.

The distances across these areas are vast although they look small on the map. Within the Coral Sea itself and close to the coast of Australia there are numerous small Islands. They are still uninhabited today, apart from a large population of sea birds, and the occasional meteorologist on Willis Island. Unmanned weather stations, beacons, and a lighthouse are located on several other islands and reefs. Occasional tropical cyclones sweep over the islands from November to April, leaving the sand and coral-based mass with little or no vegetation. To the extreme east of the area lay the Island of New Caledonia the capital of which was Nouméa. The Americans used it as a base because it had reasonably good port facilities and could be used to dominate the Coral Sea by air. Originally the French occupied it. Several of the American warships involved in this campaign were sent from Nouméa.

It is quite clear that the weather had a very significant effect on the Battle of the Coral Sea. Fletcher's ships encountered winds blowing up to 30 miles an hour from the southeast and a huge bank of cloud cover almost 300 miles wide obscured both sides from each other, hindering reconnaissance and Combat Air Patrols alike. By May 5 the cloud cover was still very low and eventually Fletcher's ships emerged from the clouds to brilliant sunshine. The same weather front that had covered Fletcher effectively did the same for the Japanese.

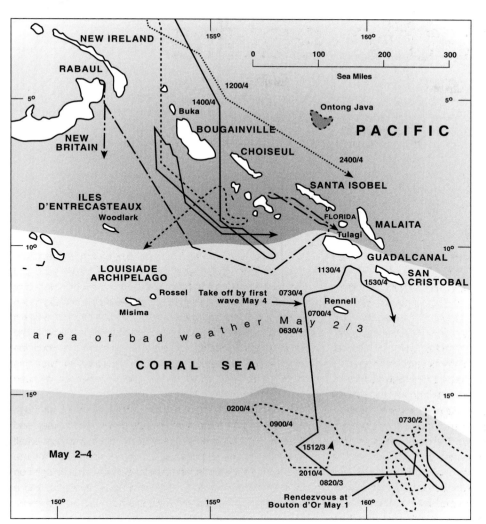

LEFT: The battle arena— the movement of forces between May 2 and 4, 1942. From the south (bottom of map) the solid line shows the path of Task Force 17; the dotted line shows the path of Task Force 11. From the north (top) the dotted lines represent the course followed by theJapanese Striking Force (above Saint Isobel) and Marumo's Support Group (to Louisade Archipeligo). The solid line shows the path of Goto's Support Group. From New Britain Admiral Shima's Naval Group moves to Tulagi and the Japanese force bound for Port Moresby heads south.

BELOW: Land-based Zero seen at Rabaul. Captured in January 1942, Rabaul gave the Japanese control of the New Guinea/Solomons area and was a major objective of the Allies. It would become pivotal in the Japanese base system. Attacked by air from October 1943, Rabaul would surrender only on September 6, 1945.

45

The Battle of the Coral Sea

Reconnaissance

The beginning of any battle starts with a reconnaissance of both sides to detect and identify the opposing forces. This is not easy on an ocean the size of the Pacific where weather fronts can dramatically affect visibility and thousands of small islands provide vantage points for hiding vessels. The Battle of the Coral Sea was punctuated by reports that were wildly exaggerated and believed when they should have been treated with some caution. Reconnaissance was exceedingly important and in some ways it worth looking at how it was done on both sides. The Japanese had an advantage in they had the Kawanishi 97K Mavis seaplane. The range of this aircraft was 4,193 miles ensuring that it could explore very large areas of ocean. The Americans did not have this sort of aircraft and relied heavily on other types that were more suited to their main combat role. The only other sorts of aircraft available to them were the bombers under McArthur's command in Australia or the 12 PBY Catalina flying boats that were based on the island of Nouméa

Comparative aircraft ranges

Aircraft	Range
Kawanishi 97 H6K Mavis	4,193 miles
Mitsubishi AM6 Zero	1,470 miles
Nakajima 97 Kate	634 miles
Aichi 99 Val	930 miles
Grumman F4F Wildcat	844 miles
Douglas SBD Dauntless	3,100 miles
Douglas TBD Devastator	652 miles

The taking of Tulagi and Fletcher's response

The Japanese occupied the island of Tulagi in the eastern Solomons with relative ease on May 3. The first the Americans knew of it was the report of a reconnaissance plane from Australia given to General MacArthur's Headquarters at 1900hrs on May 3. It was clear from this and other reports that the Japanese had been active since the morning and had, at the very least, landed troops. This gave them a distinct advantage with regard to reconnaissance in the area, since their long-range Mavis seaplanes would soon begin operating from there. American plans had not foreseen this activity and the response was something of a knee-jerk reaction.

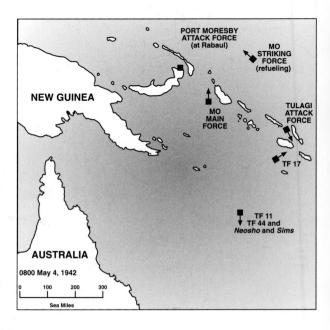

46

OPPOSITE: Position of forces at 0800hrs on May 4.

LEFT AND BELOW: Photographs and map of the attack on Tulagi—two in a sequence continued overleaf. The large land mass is Florida Island.

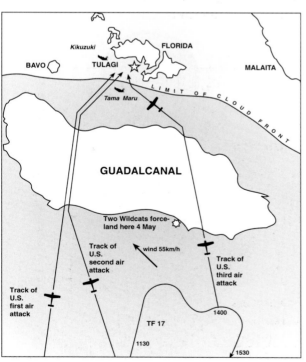

An air attack was clearly the obvious solution to this situation and, although it would betray the Allied presence in the area, it was felt that it was needed. However, there were complications. Firstly an area of bad weather had approached the Americans, it was about 300 miles wide and started from the north of the task force covering the area between it and Tulagi. While it was advantageous to mask an American approach it also hindered air operations. Since early morning both carrier air groups had been progressing to the west. It appears that communication between Fletcher and Fitch was somewhat sporadic. Refueling had begun to take place at about 1300hrs on May 3 and this had a bearing on what happened next because Fletcher was forced to use the *Yorktown* only as the basis for his attack on Tulagi. So the *Yorktown* sailed north to begin operations traveling at speeds of between 24–27 knots. At about 0600hrs on May 4 she was about 100 miles southwest of the coast of Guadalcanal. Half an hour later she headed in to the wind and launched 11 or 12 (depending on the source) Devastators of Squadron VT5 and 28 Dauntless dive-bombers of Squadrons VB5 and VS5, the former with Mk 13 torpedoes and the latter with 1,000lb bombs or in the scouting role. In addition, six Wildcat fighters were sent to escort the bombers while the remaining fighters formed a Combat Air Patrol above the carrier. Squadron VS5 under Lt. Cmdr. Burch was the first over the island at 0815hrs. Seeing the relatively undefended ships in the harbor they dived in immediately to attack and the unfortunate destroyer *Kikuzuki* bore the brunt of it, along with two small

minesweepers in the area. The *Kikuzuki* was mortally damaged by a 500lb bomb that penetrated to her engine room and the crew abandoned ship. It is normally claimed that two minesweepers were sunk and the minesweeper *Okinoshima* was certainly damaged. When the second group, VT5, arrived at the scene they launched all of their torpedoes, one of which destroyed the minesweeper *Tama Maru*. Two patrol ships were also sunk. Fifteen minutes later at 0830hrs, VB5 under Lt. Short arrived to add to the carnage but found only a couple of minor vessels to attack. The Americans all returned to the ship at around 0930hrs and immediately rearmed for a second attack. According to Morison, the second strike consisted of 27 dive-bombers and 11 torpedo planes. This second attack may have been a waste of time but it is clear that Fletcher did not believe the exaggerated claims of his pilots and therefore resolved to ensure that the target was destroyed. Having been caught off guard once, the Japanese were more prepared for the second attack and engaged the approaching U.S. planes with heavy machine-gun and anti-aircraft fire. The U.S. planes pushed through and destroyed two Kawanishi Mavis seaplanes. Again the Devastators had difficulty hitting the target in a pattern that was to be carried through to Midway and beyond, the Navy's first monoplane torpedo-armed aircraft was proving to be something of a lame duck.

A lot of effort was expended for not much return when the second wave returned to the *Yorktown* they informed Fletcher that three more seaplanes were anchored off Makambo Island in Tulagi harbor. Consequently four Wildcats were dispatched to destroy them, which they did

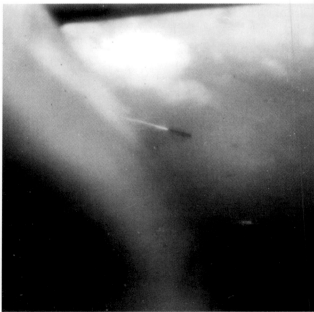

attacking the destroyer *Yuzuki* at the same time. Fletcher was still not satisfied with the third raid and decided to mount a fourth one at 1400hrs. Twenty-one Dauntless dive-bombers left the ship at 1400hrs and proceeded to make the fourth and final attack of the day. Four landing craft were sunk and not much else was achieved before the aircraft returned to the *Yorktown* at 1630hrs. Despite the victorious claims of his pilots Fletcher knew that there was precious little to cheer about. Few significant vessels had been sunk for the expenditure of a lot of effort and ammunition, though the destruction of the seaplanes had weakened the Japanese ability to carry out long-range reconnaissance. According to Japanese records they lost one destroyer, two patrol boats and a transport. In addition one transport was badly damaged, a further destroyer was damaged and a further minesweeper was damaged along with at least four seaplanes. So the first phase of the battle was over but the main combat beckoned and the Japanese now knew the Allies were in the vicinity. From the Japanese point of view, Operation MO had been detected at a vulnerable stage and they now knew there was going to be a carrier battle – the first in history.

May 5 continued with preparations for the forthcoming operation; it was a day of waiting and watching. For the Japanese their various naval groups were dispersed. The group under the control of Admiral Takagi, which included the large carriers *Zuikaku* and *Shokaku*, was refueling at North Bougainville. Goto's cruisers were further north. They were to eventually travel south through the gap between Bougainville and Choiseul Island. Takagi was informed of the American raid on Tulagi

OPPOSITE AND ABOVE: Sequence of photographs taken during the attack on Tulagi.

BELOW: Movement of forces on May 7.

at about 1200hrs and this forced him to sail southeast, close to Malaita Island.

Task Force 44

It is unusual in any battle to split one's forces in the face of an approaching enemy. Yet this is exactly what Fletcher did in the early stages of the Battle of the Coral Sea. Task

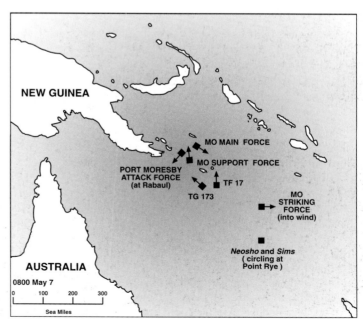

Force 44 consisted of three cruisers, USS *Chicago*, RAN *Hobart* and RAN *Australia*, and three destroyers, USS *Walke*, USS *Farragut* and USS *Perkins*. They were due to rendezvous with Fletcher's force on May 4 at 0800hrs. The Australian/American force was under the command of the British Admiral J. G. Crace. In 1939 John Crace, then Rr. Adm. R.N., was seconded by the Admiralty to take command of the Royal Australian Navy as Rr. Adm. commanding Australia Squadron.

At the outbreak of World War II, the government of Australia placed their Navy under the direction of the British Admiralty, thus giving Rr. Adm. Crace a severe organizational headache since control of the theatre resided with an organization thousands of miles away that were not fully informed of regional developments. He was on the point of asking for a transfer back to the Royal Navy when the Japanese attack on Pearl Harbor forced him to reconsider. Political considerations meant that Crace would lead the Australian and American contingent. Once the Tulagi occupation force was detected it was clear that a new rendezvous would have to be made and the *Yorktown* duly proceeded towards Tulagi whilst Crace's force, along with that of the *Lexington*, were left behind. After the sorties against Tulagi, the *Yorktown* rejoined the *Lexington* on the morning of May 5. They began sailing northwest by west on the evening of the 5th and by early morning on May 7 they were about 100 miles south of Rossel Island in the Louisade Archipelago. It was at this point that Crace was ordered to take his ships and continue northwest to the Jomard Passage. This was intended to stop the Port Moresby invasion force from coming around

the southeastern tip of New Guinea to Port Moresby by way of the passage. According to Samuel Morison, Fletcher declared that this move was intended to block the passage even if the carriers were defeated in battle by the Japanese. However, this seems unlikely as if the Japanese were successful they would surely have been able to bring enough force to bear to force the passage. By this time the Australians were accompanied by a third American destroyer, USS *Perkins*. This left Fletcher with two problems: firstly, he was reducing the anti-aircraft capability that he needed to defend his carriers against Japanese attacks and, secondly, he was exposing Task Force 44 to attacks by Japanese land-based aircraft. It has been argued that this bold move Fletcher was a tactical mistake. This is in some ways missing the point. The Japanese had a complex and multi-layered plan and had split their forces into different groups to achieve different objectives. There was no point in Fletcher defeating the carrier force if the landing force was to arrive at Port Moresby with little resistance. Therefore he did what was likely to stop them arriving at their objective by using his own blocking force. The Japanese spotted Task Force 44 at about 0810hrs and their response was not long in coming.

Crace realized that his force was liable to come under Japanese attack and formed a lozenge formation in order to protect his ships. They were traveling at 25 knots when the first attacks began between 1400hrs and 1430hrs. Commodore Dacre Smyth of the *Australia* describes them

Having been sent to the Jomard Entrance, our cruiser force was without air cover. Being under constant threat from Japanese shore-based and carrier air-craft, our position was parlous. Quoting from my mid-shipman's journal: "Radar reports from Chicago were frequent during the forenoon, and several unidentified 'planes were sighted. At 1424hrs 11 'planes appeared, and fire was opened on them. They turned away. A few minutes later, a U.S. Navy Dauntless dive-bomber appeared. It had lost its carrier, and asked for directions. As it disappeared ahead, having been told to go to Port Moresby, a for-mation of some 12 two-engined aircraft appeared on our port bow, bunched together and flying very low."

Although the first Japanese attack on Crace's force was pressed home with typical Japanese vigor it was sur-prisingly badly delivered. Torpedoes were dropped at ranges of between 1,000 and 1,500yds, after which the aircraft flew on and fired on the ships with machine guns and cannon. Three aerial torpedoes were launched at *Australia* and it seems that five of the attackers were shot down. It appears that Crace's handling of the ships, their weaving tactics and the fearful anti-aircraft barrage put the attackers off. It is worth at this point just analyzing what sort of air defense the Australian ships and their American counterparts could call upon. In 1941 the defensive armament of the cruiser *Chicago* was 8 x 5in. anti-aircraft guns, 2 x 3-pdrs and 8 machine guns. The *Australia* had 8 x 4in. anti-aircraft guns, 4 x 3-pdr anti-aircraft guns, 4 x 2-pdr pom poms, 4 x machine guns and 8 Lewis guns. The *Hobart* was similarly armed, though with fewer small caliber guns. A typical American destroyer armament such as that on the *Phelps* was 8 x 5in. 38-cal. guns, 8 x 1-pdrs and 2 machine guns. By 1942 they would all have carried more guns. Certainly the Americans were adding small caliber guns to their ships on an ad hoc basis and the trend during the war was to increase firepower as much as possible. The firing cycle of a typical 38-cal. gun was around 3–4 seconds so the rate of fire could be 15rpm. Assuming all the guns were firing this gives a possible rate of fire of 129 rounds from the heavier caliber guns, with considerably more from the smaller caliber guns. The closer the Japanese got to their targets the more guns were able to hit them and the more difficult the task became. This may explain why some of their attacks were carried out at high altitude.

The Japanese Admiral Yamada was based at Rabaul and it was he who ordered the attack from the 25th Air Group. He had been wrongly informed that there was at least one battleship with Crace's

fleet and, conscious of the threat that a ship of that size would cause to the landing at Port Moresby, he sent his fleet of bombers and torpedo planes to attack. The failure to destroy any of Crace's vessels effectively allowed the Allies to block the Jomard Passage and therefore the Japanese invasion fleet. There were in fact four separate attacks on the Task Force: the first consisted of 11 single-engined bombers then there were two successive attacks of Mitsubishi 96 Nell bombers, one of 12 planes and the other of 19, and finally, and more worrying, a group of B-26 Martin Marauders from the 19th Bombardment Group based in Townsville, Australia. The last attack prompted Crace to contact McArthur's command in protest.

The immediate consequence of the action by Task Force 44 was that Admiral Inoue gave orders to the landing group to reverse course at 0900hrs on May 7. They were to wait north of the Jomard Passage until the battle had been resolved.

The attempt to take Port Moresby required a great deal of air cover; therefore the Japanese 25th Air Group under Yamada was carrying out attacks on Port Moresby on this day. This again restricted the Japanese ability to detect the Americans, since their main scouting force was being used on this offensive mission.

LEFT: The Royal Australian Navy cruiser *Hobart*, the lighter of the two Australian cruisers involved in the battle.

BELOW: Carrier operations May 5–6.

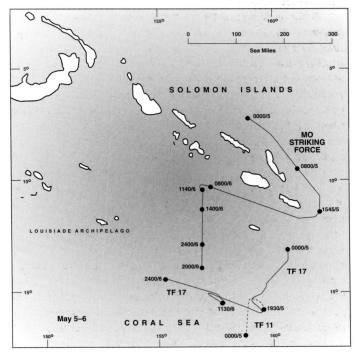

May 6 began for the Americans with the order from Adm. Fletcher to form a single group at 0730hrs that was to become known as Task Force 17. This meant that the commander of Task Force 11, Adm. Fitch, came under the direct command of Fletcher. However, as Fitch was far more experienced in the offensive use of air power he became the overall air commander at this point. The long Japanese wait for news of the Americans' location was finally broken on the morning of May 6 when a Mavis reconnaissance plane spotted the American task force and transmitted its position. It is thought that Takagi did not receive this information until the 7th, which may explain his delayed reaction to events that were about to occur.

Events of May 7

The preliminary skirmishes of the Battle of the Coral Sea were over and between May 5 and 6 a frantic search had taken place for the main battle fleets of either side. The Americans had a huge advantage in this due to their ability to decode Japanese transmissions. By 1940, the U.S. Army's Signal Intelligence Service had cracked Japan's top diplomatic code enabling U.S. forces to decipher massive amounts of high-level Japanese intelligence. Assigned the code name "Magic," this data source allowed the President and a small number of military officers access

to high-quality information concerning Japanese military activities and diplomatic policies. As with any intelligence gained from the enemy the Magic information was not always used wisely and it was difficult to judge the amount of information to use without running the risk of betraying the source. Perhaps the most serious shortfall was due to the fact this information was not analyzed in any depth or used in conjunction with material collected by independent sources and means. However, Fletcher had been informed that there were carriers in the vicinity and that Japanese forces were converging on Port Moresby. Naval Intelligence too played a large part in keeping the Americans informed of Japanese intentions. The Office of Naval Intelligence was able to read part of the Japanese Navy's JN-25 code, the one dealing with operational matters. In conjunction with the ability to read the Japanese codes the Americans could detect radio transmissions between ships and shore-based stations, the level of traffic was a good indication of imminent action.

All this meant that the Americans had an intelligence advantage that, without doubt, assisted them during the Battle of the Coral Sea. The second U.S. advantage was that their ships, or at least some of them, had radar. Early radar trials had taken place in the Caribbean in January 1939, with sets mounted on the battleships USS *New York* and USS *Texas* and aircraft could now be spotted at

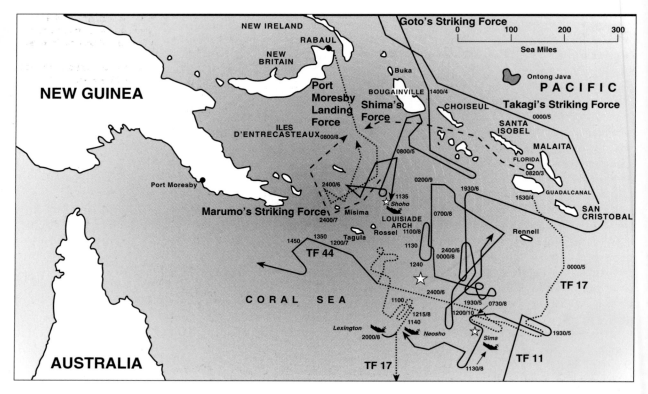

a range of 48 miles and vessels at 10 miles. It was also possible to detect surface vessel attacks at night, projectiles could be tracked in flight and radar was even used for navigation by ranging peaks on nearby islands. The Navy ordered RCA (Radio Corporation of America) to build 20 sets to their requirements. These sets were put into operational use as CXAM on capital ships, such as battleships and carriers.

Although these early radar sets were fairly primitive, their effectiveness was clearly illustrated on May 5 when a Wildcat fighter was directed onto its target by the radar of the *Yorktown*. This enabled the Wildcat to shoot down a Kawanishi H6K seaplane and delay the detection of the carrier group.

The attack on the Shoho

The *Shoho*, a Japanese escort carrier was covering the naval forces heading for the Jomard Passage during May 6, she was then ordered to wait 90 miles northeast of Deboyne Island. The *Shoho* was a light carrier that was capable of carrying 28 aircraft. She was the converted *Tsurugisaki* and was built at Yokosuka Yard. She had a displacement of 11,262 tons and was armed with 8 x 5in. 40-cal. guns and 8 x 25mm automatic anti-aircraft guns. The *Shoho* was typical of the series of converted

ships that became escort carriers in the Imperial Japanese Navy.

On the morning of May 7 just before dawn she launched four reconnaissance aircraft. These machines were intended to provide screening cover for the landing force. It just so happened that Fletcher's force now headed north into area of bad weather. This enabled him to hide from the Japanese. though the clouds were just high enough to allow him to launch some aircraft. The previously mentioned reconnaissance planes were shadowing the Americans whose Combat Air Patrol had been reinforced to try to drive them off. At 0735hrs scout sections of flight VB5 spotted the cruisers *Furutaka* and *Kinugasa*. Real contact came about at 0815hrs when two carriers and four heavy cruisers were reported about 200 miles northwest of the Task Force's position. What is interesting in this battle is the propensity of both commanders to believe that they had found the enemy. This is fully understandable but Fletcher had exercised extreme thoroughness when attacking Tulagi and yet somehow he was prepared to accept the first report of the scout confirming the Japanese Fleet's presence. This may have been because they were expecting the Japanese to be in the vicinity of the report. Both carrier crews and aircrew frantically prepared themselves for what would be the

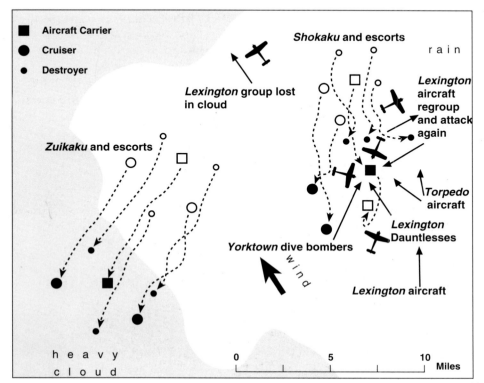

LEFT: Movement of the Japanese fleet before and after the attack on May 8.

FAR LEFT: Operations of both forces May 5–8.

first carrier against carrier attack in the Pacific War. There was at this juncture a lack of fighter cover so that of the four flights on the *Lexington* only ten were fighters, Grumman F4F Wildcats, 25 were bombers and 12 were torpedo planes. This air group carried out what was known as deferred departure, when all the aircraft formed up together before leaving for the target. They left at 0947hrs commanded by William B Ault. The *Yorktown* group consisted of eight Grumman F4F Wildcats, 25 SBD Dauntless bombers and 10 TBD Devastators, and they began to leave the ship at 0944hrs. This second group was less cohesive as the torpedo bombers had a 20-minute head start. In all 93 aircraft were winging their way to the *Shoho*. Fletcher, however, must have felt exactly like Hara when the scouting planes returned at around 1030hrs. The pilot who had reported in denied any knowledge of having seen a carrier and it was quickly discovered that his message had been wrongly coded! It was to be the army aircraft of McArthur's command that had sighted a carrier and several other ships near the original position. In addition the commander of flight VB2 of the *Lexington* also discovered the *Shoho* and escorts near the island of Tagula, so the force was redirected to that position. The Americans were also expecting a backlash once their attack had gone home so the Combat Air Patrol was stiffened by adding all the Dauntlesses on anti-torpedo aircraft patrol to the protective screen above the fleet. This was not unusual since the Dauntlesses were used for scouting, bombing and even as fighters when the need arose.

The *Shoho* was commanded by Capt. Izawa Ishinosuke who was at that moment preparing for an attack himself, even though his aircraft were being recovered. The launch of the attack planes ordered by Inoue was complicated by the fact that the *Shoho* was a converted depot ship and so had design limitations. Lt. Cmdr. Ault and the three command Dauntlesses of the *Lexington* group carried out the first attack on her at around 1107hrs near Misima Island. There were four Japanese cruisers covering the *Shoho*: the *Kakao*, *Furutaka*, *Aoba* and *Kinugasa*, as well as the destroyer *Sazanami*. Together they were able to muster a decent anti-aircraft barrage, there was also a small Japanese Combat Air Patrol, but this had been dispersed by the need to chase other aircraft notably VS2. The first attacks all missed the target partly due to a sharp turn to port made by Capt. Izawa. The next group to attack was Dixon's VS2, who had been pursued by fighters and whose dives were interrupted by them. The *Shoho* continued to turn to port and, although scouts claimed she was hit there was no confirmation. At this point three further fighters were launched from the *Shoho*.

The next wave came in under the command of Lt. Cmdr. Hamilton:

Lt. Cmdr. Weldon Hamilton, the dive-bomber skipper, was at the front of his formation, which had climbed up to 15,000 feet and was slightly ahead and above Dixon's scout bombers, who were at 12,000. Underneath these two groups were Brett's torpedo

planes. The fighters split up, four pairs in the high-level group flying slightly above and behind Hamilton, and the other four idling along with the torpedo squadron. "We began from 16,500 feet and pushed over in our dive at 12,000. The Jap was exactly downwind as I nosed down, simplifying my problem tremendously. My bomb, which was the first 1,000-pdr to hit struck in the middle of the flight deck's width, just abaft amidships. As I looked back the entire after-portion of the flight deck was ablaze and pouring forth heavy smoke."

A second bomb hit the *Shoho* further forward just after Hamilton's attack causing explosions and confusion in the fires and wreckage. One can see the amount courage needed for this kind of attack when one considers the interview with the experience of Ens. Leppla.

When I looked into the cockpit I found that other shots had gone through the Plexiglas cockpit covers, missed the pilot and gunner by inches, and then completely smashed some of the instrument board. One bullet tore off the heel of the pilot's shoe, and another, after coming through the plane and buzzing around the cockpit like a bee went through the leg of his flying suit and was found stuck in the knee of his trousers. *(Queen of the Flatops)*

The next attack was from the torpedo bombers approaching from the southwest and they decided to split

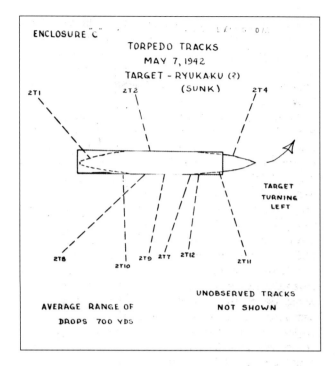

ABOVE: Although named as *Ryukaku*, this shows the hits on *Shoho* that led to its demise.

BELOW AND BELOW LEFT: A sequence of photographs (continued overleaf) showing the *Shoho* taking hits during the battle, May 7. The photographs are by an aircraft off USS *Lexington*. Note the TBD-1 visible to the right of the large splash in the photograph on page 54.

their forces and go at the ship simultaneously. This meant that torpedoes could be launched from either side of the ship preventing it from maneuvering away. Because of their low-level attack they were vulnerable to anti-aircraft fire and the cruisers were putting up a wall of lead. The release height for the American torpedoes was only 100ft—it was a decidedly risky proposition. Squadron VT2 were the first in to attack from the stern and the torpedo of Lt. Thornhill hit the *Shoho* on her port side. VT2 probably hit the *Shoho* five times, over 5,500lb of explosive that destroyed her engine room and tore holes in her side. She began to lose speed and, whilst fires were raging on her decks her below decks area was awash with water.

The *Yorktown* group was 15 minutes behind the *Lexington* group and they proceeded to give the coup de grace to the ship. Within five minutes she was a steaming, burning wreck. Even after this she had to endure a further torpedo attack from VT5 of the *Yorktown*, who may well have been better directed against the cruisers all of whom seem to have escaped from the encounter unscathed. The order to abandon the *Shoho* was given at 1131hrs and the ship sank at 1135hrs. Only about 100 men of the crew survived picked up by the destroyer *Sazanami*. The rest of the battle dissolved into a series fighter combats and the attacking planes finally assembled at 1140hrs for the journey back to their respective carriers. At 1210hrs Cmdr. R. E. Dixon of squadron VS2 of the *Lexington* sent the

signal "Scratch one flat top! Signed Bob" to the Task Force. But, and it was big but, the relief that the carrier commanders felt at that moment was to be short lived. The Americans had actually identified the *Shoho* as a carrier of the Ryujo class and one can still see captions on official U.S. photographs quoting her as the *Ryukaku*.

There were others who did not make it back to the ship Edward Allen and Ens. Quigley were hit by anti-aircraft fire whilst in a dive and were forced to land on Rossel Island, only being rescued some 18 days later.

"I was stunned a little but the water coming in revived me. We got the rubber boat out and took the chart board. We rowed for 45 minutes but got nowhere cos the current was too strong." They saw an outrigger and three of the wildest natives you can imagine.

The end of this attack was followed by the long return flight to the U.S. carriers, who promptly received them at 1335hrs. Three aircraft had been lost during this attack. In his usual thorough way Fletcher was already thinking of a second attack. The aircraft were prepared and ready to go an hour later but the order was never given. It seems that a combination of factors stayed his hand at that time.

Far Left and Left: Two more views of the crippled *Shoho*. TBD Devastators can be seen in the photograph on page 56.

The loss of the Neosho and the Sims

Fletcher had detached the destroyer *Sims* and the oiler *Neosho* on May 6 to go to their next refueling station, they arrived there at about 0810hrs the following morning. It was at this time that they saw two approaching aircraft. Takagi's force had been making a search southwards since the early hours of the morning. Takagi did not know the whereabouts of the American carriers so he was moving westward covering the MO invasion group. At 0600hrs Hara's carriers launched 12 Type 97 aircraft to search for the U.S. fleet. The planes were looking for the Americans in a southerly direction to a range of about 250 miles away from their carriers. After one and a half-hour's search the *Zuikaku* received a message from the eastern-most aircraft that he had seen an aircraft carrier and a cruiser. In fact it was the *Neosho* and the *Sims*. Aircraft were already being prepared for a possible action and efforts were redoubled to make sure they could catch the Americans. A further aircraft was sent to keep contact with the ships while the rest were readied for the attack. The first wave of Kate bombers took off at 0800hrs. In all the attack consisted of 78 planes: 36 dive-bombers, 24 torpedo planes and 18 fighters under the control of Lt. Cmdr. Kakuichi Takahashi. The search aircraft from the carriers had not been the only ones looking for the American fleet. At 0815hrs Task force 17 was found south of Rossel Island. Once this message was received further confirmation came at 0830hrs. Both sightings were very close to each other and it was thought that the Japanese striking force was sending its aircraft to Rossel Island when in fact they were heading south.

The attacking Japanese forces arrived at 0935hrs over the spot where the American ships had been seen. After a short search only a solitary destroyer and tanker were found rather than a grand U.S. fleet. The search appeared to be fruitless and, rather than return empty-handed, Kakuichi decided to attack the solitary ships. At 0945hrs the first wave of aircraft screamed towards their targets, but with little success. The *Sims* began weaving in order to avoid bombs; the *Neosho* followed about a mile behind. Kakuichi did not arrive over the scene until a little later with 36 dive-bombers. The *Sims* was forced to turn and support the *Neosho* with her anti-aircraft guns, thus exposing her rear to attack. The skill of the Aichi Val pilots was decisive and they hit the *Sims* with three armor-piercing bombs that exploded in her engine room. This left her motionless and with no means of escape. The following description was given by the survivors after the action:

Four planes broke off from one wave of *Neosho* attackers and directed their attack at the *Sims*, diving on her in succession from astern. All of these planes were single-motored, had fixed landing gear, and had a silhouette similar to that of Japanese dive-bombers. The first released a bomb which landed in the water about amidships to port; the second released a bomb which landed on Number Two Torpedo Mount and exploded in the forward engine room; the third released a bomb which apparently hit the after upper deck house and went down through diagonally forward, exploding in the after engine room; the fourth plane is believed to have made a direct hit on Number Four Gun, but this cannot be definitely established. Numbers Three and Four Mounts and the after 20mm guns were put out of commission by the bomb hits, but the forward mounts in local control and one 20mm gun continued firing at the planes until all of them were out of gun range. The total number of rounds fired by the *Sims* cannot be ascertained, but one survivor states that over 200 rounds were fired from Number Two Mount alone. During this last attack, the paint on the barrel of Number One Mount blistered and caught fire; the crew, however, continued to fire with the complete length of the barrel in flames. Several planes were brought down by gunfire during this attack. *Neosho* survivors told *Sims* survivors that the planes that attacked the *Sims* were never seen to emerge from the blast of their bomb explosions. It is believed that the bombs dropped were about 500lb size.

CSM R. J. Dicken had to swim out to the boat from the ship and his comments were noted in the same report quoted above

He noted that there was no oil on the water at this time. On taking charge of the boat Dicken proceeded around the bow to the lee side of the ship aft. As the motor whaleboat approached, the ship seemed to break amidships and start to sink slowly. The stern went under first and appeared to draw the bow aft, pulling it down stern first. All hands began abandoning ship in life jackets, swimming for the rafts. Just as the water level reached the top of the stack and began running down into it, a terrific explosion occurred. What remained of the ship was lifted 10 to 15ft out of the water, and the surface of the water around the ship was covered with oil. This great explosion was followed by another smaller one, which survivors definitely identified as a depth charge explosion. The remaining forward section then settled slowly, sinking in about five minutes. One man who couldn't swim was seen hanging onto the anchor until the stem disappeared into the water.

Survivors estimate that the ship sank in about 15 to 20 minutes after receiving the first direct hit. Under conditions of stress such as existed at the time, minutes would seem like hours and it is quite possible that the ship sank much more rapidly than these men estimate.
(*Naval Intelligence Combat Reports*)

The *Neosho* did not long survive the destruction of the *Sims* as she received seven bomb strikes and one aircraft that crashed into her stern and set the ship alight. There were many efforts of heroism during the attacks on the *Neosho*. Chief Watertender Oscar Verner Peterson was a case in point, he literally burnt himself to death to try and save the ship. Without assistance because of injuries to the other members of his repair party and severely wounded himself, Peterson closed the bulkhead stop valves and in so doing received additional burns that resulted in his death. He was awarded the Medal of Honor posthumously for his efforts.

The *Neosho* did not sink straight away and, even though she had lost her rudder, she drifted for four days until the destroyer *Henley* from the salvage group found her.

Immediately prior to the attack on the *Sims* and *Neosho*, the Japanese admirals realized that they had made a serious error. They had dispatched a large attacking force onto a pair of vessels that were not worth the effort. Although destroying the two ships was militarily useful, it was clear that valuable time had been lost. Now that the main American force was located the aircraft had to return, rearm and get organized for the major assault. A large force such as the Japanese had dispatched was almost impossible to recall. The cost in ammunition, fuel and other resources was also very high. Although it was surprising that Admiral Hara did not get more confirmation before launching such a large attack, this was not the only mistake of the day. Around 1500hrs a reconnaissance report was received that indicated that the U.S. Task Force had altered course and headed south. At this point the Americans were believed to be 330–360 miles to the west of the Japanese Fleet. Takagi knew that if he was to launch an afternoon raid he might well steal a march on the Americans, but it would mean returning in the dark, a factor that would be significant later in the battle and that was to be significant for later developments. At 1630hrs in the afternoon of May 7, 12 Aichi Type 99 dive-bombers and 15 Kate Type 97 torpedo planes left the carriers on yet another sortie. They were expected to make a three and a half-hour flight to the target. Considering the weather front that the Americans were engulfed in it would be a matter of enormous skill or complete luck if they found the American ships at all. According to several authors, it was at the limit of their search pattern that they realized that they were not going to find the Americans. What they did not realize was that they were much closer than they thought, they had been detected on the *Lexington*'s radar at about 48 miles out. Obviously the Americans had a Combat Air Patrol on station, but they were low on fuel and so there was a frantic scramble to get more fighters aloft when the Japanese were spotted by the radar. The first unit attacked was Lt. Cmdr. Shimazaki's group of nine Type 97 Kate torpedo planes from the *Zuikaku* and in the ensuing melee attacks five Japanese aircraft were shot down for the loss of one American plane. These fighter aircraft were recalled to refuel and a second wave of seven further Wildcats from VF42 under Lt. Flately were dispatched. This group encountered Kate torpedo-bombers from the *Shokaku* commanded by Lt. Ichihara Tatsuo. In this battle the Japanese lost a further two planes and one severely damaged (which eventually ditched) whilst the Americans lost another Wildcat piloted by ensign Lt. Knox.

BELOW AND BELOW RIGHT: Two drawings showing the tactical dispositions of Japanese forces during the battle—*Shoho* and escorts (below) and *Zuikaku* and *Shokaku*.

A further Aichi Val was shot down but the light was failing fast and soon it was almost impossible to see. After taking a severe mauling from the Americans, the Japanese decided to jettison their weapons and returned to their own carriers. They had taken a risk in sending the bombers and torpedo planes without fighter cover and had paid the price. Between 1830hrs and 1845hrs, the American fighters returned to their ships while the Japanese fled back to theirs. Night had closed in and the Americans were clearly having trouble recalling their planes. At about 1850 four additional aircraft appeared apparently trying to land on the *Yorktown*, one of them signaling with an Aldiss lamp. These aircraft turned out to be four extremely disorientated Japanese aircraft, which were immediately set upon by a Wildcat that was near to the *Yorktown*. The Japanese were forced away but the situation had caused some alarm and the pilots of two Wildcats, Ens. W. W. Barnes and Dick Wright, were both fired upon in the act of landing.

Events of May 8

After all the events of the 7th, May 8 would be a day of reckoning, or at least that was how it seemed to many of the officers on both sides that day. Both had made less than spectacular attacks on bogus targets and both

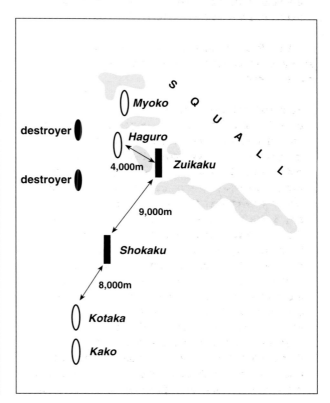

realized that it was still possible to strike the killing blow if the opportunity was given to them. The weather was clear and there was a sense that major action was imminent. The Japanese were 100 miles east-southeast of Rossell Island going north. Fletcher and Task Force 17 were 200 miles southwest of this position heading south. In terms of weather the tables had been turned; the Americans were in clear daylight whereas the Japanese were happily concealed in cloud cover. They also changed their formation; each carrier was escorted by two heavy cruisers and two or three destroyers but the two groups sailed about 10 miles apart. This was done so that if one were detected the other might not be as well and this is exactly what happened. Very early in the day Hara had decided to carry out a search and at 0615hrs sent seven planes off to search in a southerly direction to a radius of 200 miles. Conveniently for the Japanese, Hara had the assistance of the land-based aircraft of the 5th Air Attack force from Rabaul and Tulagi. Three Kawanishi's from Tulagi were to cover the northern Coral Sea and four other land-based planes were to look at the Louisades. This airborne reconnaissance was absolutely essential and whoever spotted the other's fleet first would have the advantage of first strike. Both forces were making course changes: the Americans headed west at 0116hrs, whilst the Japanese headed southwest at 0700hrs before Hara launched an attack group of planes at 0822hrs to search the area in which he expected the Americans to be. Fletcher's force now consisted of five heavy cruisers, seven destroyers and his two carriers. According to Morison both sides had almost equivalent numbers of aircraft: 121 Japanese and 122 American. This is not the whole story and Lundstrom states that there were only 95 aircraft available to the Japanese at the time of the battle, consisting of 37 fighters, 33 dive-bombers and 25 torpedo carrying planes. The Americans were also keen to send up aircraft to track down the Japanese fleet and at 0625hrs the *Lexington* launched 18 aircraft with that express purpose. Incredibly, both sides spotted each other almost simultaneously. At 0833hrs a Japanese spotter plane relayed a message that it had spotted the American carriers. This message was intercepted by the Americans and translated so that they too knew they were being sought out, whilst Lt. J. G. Smith saw the Japanese preparing for takeoff at roughly the same time and gave the composition of the Japanese force. Lt. Cmdr. R. E. Dixon of VS2 flew out to try to maintain this contact but failed to find Smith. He eventually found the Japanese at 0930hrs and realized that the location of the ships was wrong. He maintained contact for another hour and a quarter. Exactly 23 minutes after the first sighting the Americans gave the order to launch their

attacks. The planes of the *Yorktown* left at 0915hrs and arrived at the target at 1100hrs. As usual the Dauntlesses, flying faster than the lumbering Devastators, were first to arrive flying at about 17,000 feet. At this point the *Shokaku* was visible to the attackers but the *Zuikaku* was not as she had been hidden under the clouds. The *Yorktown*'s bombers were the first to attack the *Shokaku* when VT5 attacked at 1100hrs. The attack of the torpedo bombers initiated by Lt. Cmdr. Taylor was a failure as the pilots launched their torpedoes too far away from the carrier. As a result no explosions were seen and this left the Americans with just the dive-bombers to carry out the attack. They succeeded where the torpedo bombers had failed and two hits were made on the *Shokaku*; one on the starboard side of the flight deck and the other on the stern. This latter bomb destroyed the engine repair workshop on the lower flight deck. As all of this was happening the fighters were engaged in a struggle either to support the attacks or to counteract the Japanese air patrols.

More torpedo-carrying aircraft then arrived from the *Lexington*, four Dauntlesses from VS2 and six Wildcats from VF2. This second attack was organized by Cmdr. W Ault, the Air Group commander who was missing believed dead after the battle. The cloud cover that hid the *Zuikaku* also gave some vital cover to the U.S. attack. As the torpedo bombers approached the *Shokaku*, followed by the Dauntlesses, six of the escorting fighters peeled off to engage in a duel with an equal number of Japanese fighters. This left the *Shokaku* stripped of defensive cover and completely exposed to torpedo attack.

The *Lexington* flight, which flew off ten minutes later, ran into confusion. The three Widcat fighter escorts supporting 18 Dauntlesses of VB2 got lost in cloud and returned to the Lexington without doing anything. For some reason they had been given the wrong destination information and therefore were unable to find the Japanese, after circling for a while they were forced to jettison their weapons and return to the carrier. The torpedo flight VT2 was also directed onto the initial position of the Japanese fleet as first sighted and therefore could not find them. They then flew in a box search and eventually found the Japanese at 1140hrs. Again the Devastators released their weapons from an approach from 6,000ft allowing the Japanese commanders time to maneuver away from the torpedoes. The dive-bombers fared little better, landing just one further bomb on the *Shokaku*. This hit her on the starboard bow starting a fire and preventing her from launching aircraft. 108 Japanese sailors were killed and 40 wounded in this attack. Because she could not launch aircraft some of her planes were transferred to the *Zuikaku*.

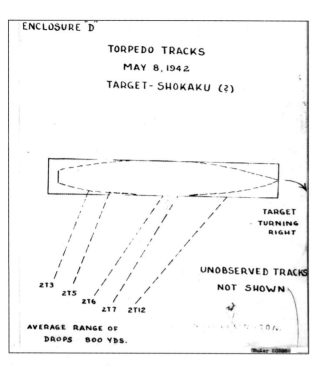

ENCLOSURE "D"

TORPEDO TRACKS

MAY 8, 1942

TARGET - SHOKAKU (?)

TARGET
TURNING
RIGHT

UNOBSERVED TRACKS

NOT SHOWN

2T3
2T5
2T6
2T7 2T12

AVERAGE RANGE OF
DROPS 800 YDS.

BuAer 20286

As soon as the Japanese ships saw the torpedo bombers they went into a zigzag movement to spoil the aim of the torpedo bombers and, once again, no successful hits were recorded. The dive-bombers, however, were much more successful in a task that was daunting to say the least in the face of hostile aircraft and anti-aircraft batteries. The citation of Lt. Powers of the *Lexington*, who was killed in a dive-bombing attack on this day, gives an impression of the situation in the skies over the *Shokaku* on May 8.

He led his section of dive-bombers down to the target from an altitude of 18,000ft, through a wall of bursting anti-aircraft shells and into the face of enemy fighter planes. Again, completely disregarding the safety altitude and without fear or concern for his safety, Lt. Powers courageously pressed home his attack, almost to the very deck of an enemy carrier and did not release his bomb until he was sure of a direct hit. He was last seen attempting recovery from his dive at the extremely low altitude of 200ft, and amid a terrific barrage of shell and bomb fragments,

ABOVE LEFT: The torpedo tracks that led to hits on *Shokaku*, May 8.

LEFT AND OVERLEAF: The start of a sequence of photographs taken by aircraft from *Yorktown* of *Shokaku* under attack, maneuvering in a vain attempt to evade the bombs. See also pages 62–67.

smoke, flame and debris from the stricken vessel.
(*Medal of Honor citation*)

The Japanese authors Hata and Izawa claim that the *Shokaku* Combat Air Patrol shot down 21 torpedo bombers and dive-bombers during this attack. Petty Officer Takeo Miyazawa is said to have shot down one torpedo bomber and crashed into another to prevent the destruction of the carrier itself. They also claim that the ten-plane fighter compliment of the *Zuikaku* did similar execution destroying a total of 11 bombers/torpedo planes and 13 fighters. These figures seem a trifle fanciful when one considers the total number of losses recorded by the Americans.

The Japanese had actually launched their attack before the Americans, with their attack force consisting of 70 aircraft. The Americans expected an attack at and had estimated that the Japanese planes would arrive at about 1100hrs. In fact they turned up about five minutes before predicted when the radar of the *Lexington* saw a group of aircraft 70 miles to the northeast. Unfortunately, one patrol had just been recovered and there were only eight aircraft on Combat Air Patrol. They were also low on fuel and so had to be kept near the carriers and could not be vectored out to the Japanese attackers. The carriers immediately changed course to 125 degrees and sped up. A further nine Wildcats were launched of which five were sent to intercept the Japanese. It was a case of too little too late and they arrived at their attack point at the wrong height to make a successful intercept, while the Japanese fighter escort also made it difficult for them to molest the attacking bombers. Things were desperate and the shining example of this is the fact that 23 Dauntlesses were in the air being used as fighters. Coming in from the northeast the Japanese torpedo bombers came in on both bows of the *Lexington* in a textbook attack. They launched their torpedoes at a distance of about 1,300yds and at between 50 and 200ft. The effectiveness of the American 5in. anti-aircraft fire was

ABOVE AND ABOVE RIGHT: Two more views of the sequence of photographs of *Shokaku*.

RIGHT: Movement of USS *Lexington* and *Yorktown* on May 8.

demonstrated when one of the aircraft disintegrated into a ball of flame throwing the airmens' bodies into the sea. However, whichever way the *Lexington* moved it was difficult to avoid torpedoes, which is exactly what the Japanese had hoped for. Lt. Cmdr. Paul D Stroop had been up since 0330hrs that morning:

We began seeing enemy aircraft overhead and they came down in a very well coordinated attack, with torpedo planes and dive-bombers. I can remember standing on the bridge and watching the enemy dive-bombers come down. These were fixed landing gear dive-bombers, [Aichi99 Val] and you were convinced the pilot in the plane had the bridge of your ship right in his sight. Fortunately, they were not strafing, because if they had been, I'm sure that they would have made the top-side untenable.

Of the torpedo attack he stated "if you were

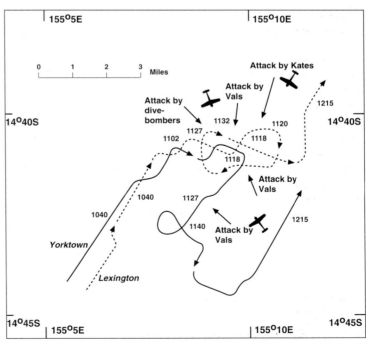

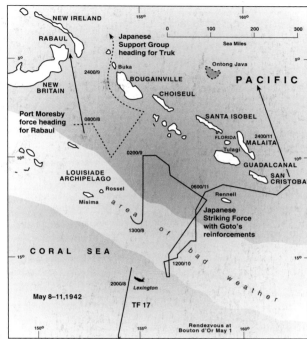

ABOVE: Movements of the fleets May 8–11.

LEFT: Another view in the sequence of photographs of the *Shokaku*.

in the general vicinity of a hit, you could be hurt; the shock to the deck you were standing on was enough to break people's legs if a torpedo hit in the general vicinity."

Accordingly, one torpedo hit the port side of the ship at 1120hrs and a second hit the port side opposite the bridge. The attack was extremely well coordinated with both bombers and torpedoes hitting at similar times.

While all of this was occurring the *Yorktown* was also receiving unwelcome attention. At almost the same time as the *Lexington* was hit three torpedoes were launched on her port quarter. She was more maneuverable than the *Lexington* and was thus able to avoid the torpedoes, which in fact only came from one side. However, she was attacked about five minutes later by dive-bombers and one of their projectiles hit her near the bridge penetrating down to the fourth deck and causing serious casualties, though this did not stop her from carrying out operations.

A complete description of the damage to the *Yorktown* makes sobering reading:

The bomb which struck the *Yorktown*'s flight deck penetrated a vertical distance of 50ft from the point

67

FAR RIGHT: *Lexington* seen from *Yorktown* on May 8—one of a sequence of photographs taken of CV-2—see following pages.

RIGHT: The torpedo attack on TF17, 1118–1121hrs, May 8.

BELOW RIGHT: The dive bombing of TF17, 1121–1124hrs, May 8.

In these drawings, the ships are identified by pennant numbers as follows:

AIRCRAFT CARRIERS
CV-2 *Lexington*
CV-5 *Yorktown*

HEAVY CRUISERS
CA-27 USS *Chester*
   (Northampton class)
CA-32 USS *New Orleans*
   (New Orleans class)
CA-33 USS *Portland*
   (Portland class)
CA-34 USS *Astoria*
   (New Orleans class)
CA-36 USS *Minneapolis*
   (New Orleans class)

DESTROYERS
DD-349 USS *Dewey*
   (Farragut class)
DD-355 USS *Aylwin*
   (Farragut class)
DD-360 USS *Phelps* (Porter
   class)
DD-411 USS *Anderson* (Sims
   class)
DD-412 USS *Hammann*
   (Sims class)
DD-414 USS *Russell*
   (Sims class)
DD-417 USS *Morris*
   (Sims class)

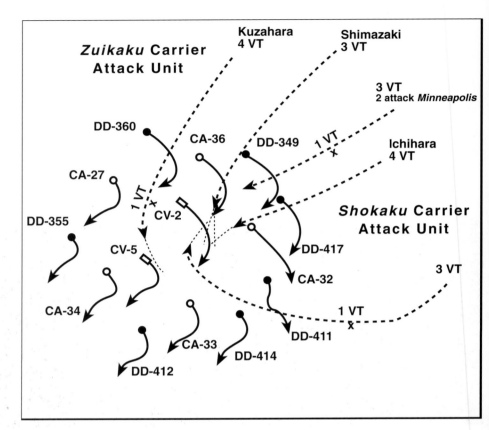

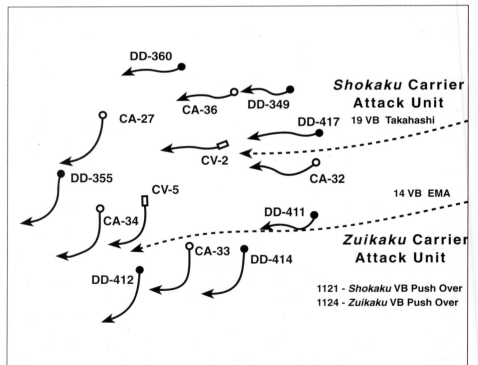

of impact to the point of detonation, piercing a total thickness of 1.68in. of steel deck plating. The hole in the flight deck was clean. The holes in the hangar and second decks were jagged and somewhat larger. The ship's shell was not punctured. The flight and galley decks were not harmed, but the hangar deck was bulged across its entire breadth from frame No. 100 to frame No. 115. A hole 4ft in diameter was blown up through the second deck 8ft inboard of the bomb impact hole, and the entire deck in the marine living compartment was bulged upward. Also, the transverse bulkheads of this compartment were badly bulged forward and aft. However, they did not rupture, and all doors remained secure, though severely warped. When the bomb hit the second deck it pierced the general lighting and battle light and power circuits for the damaged area, causing short circuits. Several people in the fire parties were shocked, one seriously. A hole 6ft in diameter was blown out of the third deck, with the deck turned and peeled back over an area of 35 square feet. The entire deck in compart-ment C-301-1L was bulged upward, and the ship's-service store and office, soda fountain, engineer's

office, and laundry issue room were wrecked.

The fourth deck was not ruptured but was dished downward over an area of 40 square feet. The inboard bulkhead of the forward engine room access truck, and the after bulkhead of the laundry storeroom were shattered. Two watertight doors were severely damaged and a large hatch cover was thrown about 15ft up into the No. 2 elevator pit. The transverse bulkheads and doors joining four compartments were blown out.
(*Naval Intelligence Combat Reports*)

All of this is nothing compared to the difficulty that the *Lexington* was in. Unbelievably the attacks had lasted just 25 minutes. The problem was that the destruction unleashed on either side had made the rest of the day a struggle for survival, especially on board the *Lexington*. Sailors are trained to deal with fire. It is the one great threat to a ship carrying huge amounts of explosives and fuel and the response aboard the *Lexington* was magnificent. She had received hits from at least two torpedoes and four bombs. One of these bombs was apparently a 1,000lb device that had hit the after end of the port forward gun gallery. Its impact killed the crew of the No. 6 gun as well as a number of men on nearby guns. Several men also were killed inboard in the main passageway on the main deck; this was because the bomb was thought to have set of a stack of 5in. gun rounds in the vicinity. Fire broke out on the gun gallery, in the admiral's cabin and the surrounding area. The second large bomb to hit was a 500lb weapon that hit the gig boat pocket on the port side killing many men. A third and considerably smaller bomb hit and exploded inside the stack. Initially it was believed that more than two torpedoes had hit the ship, then it was realized that two large caliber bombs had hit near the port side aft. Flying fragments from one or more near hits aft on the starboard side also killed and injured several machine gunners in the sky aft and the after signal station.

The *Lexington* had received some punishment but it was thought that she could be saved, although immediately after the battle she had a 6–7 degree list to port. It was reported that three of her boiler rooms were full of water and that there were three large fires raging. In fact by 1230hrs the fires were out and everybody on board thought that the worst was over, when a huge explosion rocked the ship at 1247hrs. It turned out that the pipes that carried petrol around the ship had been shaken and that sparks generated by a generator rotor had set the whole thing off. Explosions then began to rock the ship in stages. The communications links around the ship were damaged and this prevented one group of firefighters from finding out what the other was doing

Adm. Fletcher reassumed tactical command from Fitch at 1510hrs but, following the explosions on board the great carrier, time was slipping away. It was planned to take her serviceable planes aboard the *Yorktown* and send her back to Pearl Harbor for repairs quickly as possible. One of the problems was that the firefighters inside the ship needed breathing apparatus and many of the men not so equipped could not assist in the difficult areas without being overcome by fumes. Cmdr. Seligman described the events on board at the time:

Lt. Cmdr. Edward J. O'Donnell, the gunnery officer, had procured two additional hoses from aft. These were led into the scuttles of the 5in. ammunition hoist to starboard, and the last available hose was led into the dumb waiter of the food distribution room in an attempt to flood the C.P.O. [Chief Petty Officer] country. Good pressure was maintained on these hoses for a short time and it was hoped that sufficient water could be gotten below to flood the area on fire forward of the quarter deck and check the spread of the blaze. Under existing conditions it was impossible to combat it otherwise. "I ordered life rafts made ready and preparations made to abandon ship," Captain Sherman related. "Fire

fighting efforts were still being made until the engineering plant was abandoned, when all water pressure was gone."
(*Naval Intelligence Combat Reports*)

It was at this point that Sherman requested assistance of the destroyers through Adm. Fitch. The Admiral directed destroyers to come alongside, as it was time to get the personnel at risk off the ship. The destroyers provided fire hoses and water to combat the fires while the crew climbed down ropes off the ship. The destroyer *Morris* risked a great deal by coming as close as she did. But it was all to no avail: the torpedo warheads were threatened by the fire and, at a temperature of 60 degrees centigrade, the threat was too much. At 1630hrs the ship stopped. At 1830hrs the torpedo warheads finally exploded. The ship was abandoned with Sherman and his entourage the last to leave. It was the destroyer *Phelps* that finally finished off the *Lexington* by firing four torpedoes at her. She sank at around 2000hrs in the evening taking her remaining aircraft and deceased crew with her.

But what of the other ships belonging to the carrier groups? The destroyers and cruiser whose job it was to defend the great carriers. Luckily for them, the Japanese were not interested in destroying these ships as the carriers were the greater prizes. In terms of their response we can look at the views of the commander of the *Portland*, Capt. Perlman who stated that:

All fire, except in the instance of one torpedo plane that was shot down approaching the *Yorktown*, was "generally without damaging effect, inasmuch as lead-offs were too small and planes were out of effective range. However, the volume of fire was apparently disconcerting to the pilots, who released torpedoes against the *Yorktown* considerably earlier than they did against the *Lexington*."

Captain Perlman described three "phases" of the action. The second began about 1120 and consisted of a coordinated enemy torpedo plane and dive-bomber attack on the *Yorktown*. The *Portland* fired on these planes with all bearing guns without any effect other than a possible element of disturbance. The third phase consisted of uncoordinated attacks by single dive-bombers from several directions. During this phase two planes diving either at the *Portland* or

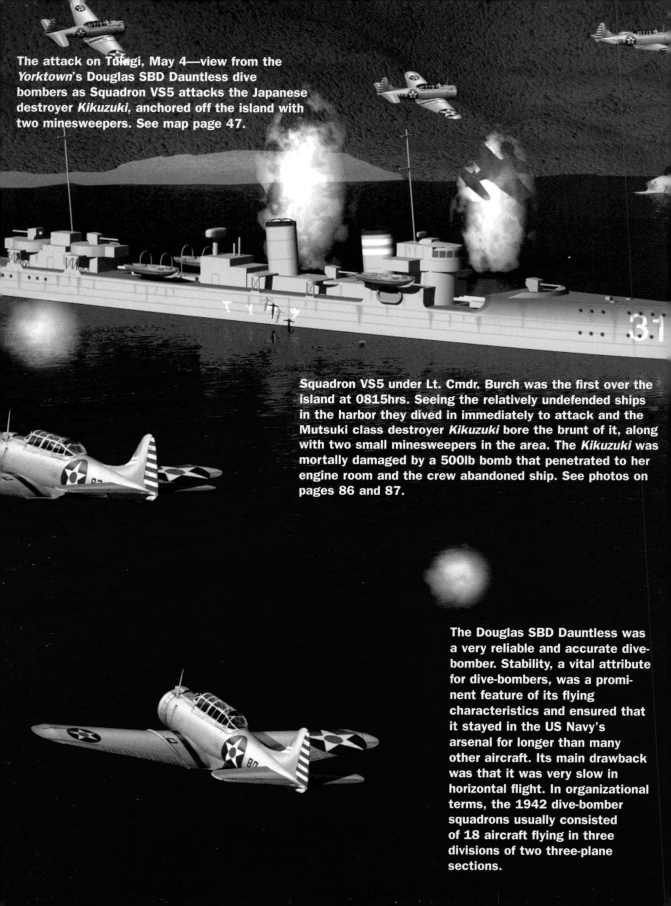

The attack on Tulagi, May 4—view from the *Yorktown*'s Douglas SBD Dauntless dive bombers as Squadron VS5 attacks the Japanese destroyer *Kikuzuki*, anchored off the island with two minesweepers. See map page 47.

Squadron VS5 under Lt. Cmdr. Burch was the first over the island at 0815hrs. Seeing the relatively undefended ships in the harbor they dived in immediately to attack and the Mutsuki class destroyer *Kikuzuki* bore the brunt of it, along with two small minesweepers in the area. The *Kikuzuki* was mortally damaged by a 500lb bomb that penetrated to her engine room and the crew abandoned ship. See photos on pages 86 and 87.

The Douglas SBD Dauntless was a very reliable and accurate dive-bomber. Stability, a vital attribute for dive-bombers, was a prominent feature of its flying characteristics and ensured that it stayed in the US Navy's arsenal for longer than many other aircraft. Its main drawback was that it was very slow in horizontal flight. In organizational terms, the 1942 dive-bomber squadrons usually consisted of 18 aircraft flying in three divisions of two three-plane sections.

It is normally claimed that two minesweepers were sunk by VS5 as well as the *Kikuzuki*. The minesweeper *Okinoshima* was certainly damaged. The second group, VT5 sank the minesweeper *Tama Maru* and two patrol ships.

the *Yorktown* were observed to turn away when engaged by one 1.1in. mount and four 20mm. guns. Both planes departed smoking. Two other planes, retiring on a course opposite to that of the cruiser at an altitude of 4,000ft, were fired on by one 5in. battery but escaped.
(*Naval Intelligence Combat Reports*)

The combat reports from the *Hamman* report that two aircraft were shot down during the action. The *Chester* reported three and the *Russell* two definites. So the anti-aircraft fire may have accounted for seven enemy planes, apart from those damaged by the *Yorktown* herself. The reports themselves indicate a degree of doubt. In terms of the *Lexington* group the *Minneapolis* claimed three shot down whilst the *New Orleans* did not claim any because she was about 4,300yds away from the *Lexington* and therefore was firing at extreme range. Capt. Good of the *New Orleans* stated "That the 5-inch guns were entirely too slow in train and elevation to effectively keep on fast moving dive-bombers or gliding torpedo planes," and that "the need for remote control of 1.1in. and 20mm. mounts is more apparent than ever." The only casualty aboard the *New Orleans* occurred among the crew of 1.1in. mount on the fantail, which was continuously wet from spray and occasional green seas. At one point, this gun was completely submerged, and the crew narrowly escaped being washed overboard. During the course of this one man received a broken nose. The Americans may have thought that their fire was not good enough but to the Japanese it was terrifying, as Capt. Shigekazu Shimazaki said after the battle, "We encountered a veritable wall of anti-aircraft fire. The aircraft carriers and their escorts darkened the sky with their tracer bullets, shells and shrapnel. It seemed impossible that we could survive such a stream of anti-aircraft gunfire."

Of the destroyers, the *Phelps* claimed one aircraft, the *Dewey* three and the *Morris* two, although it is entirely possible that claims were made from multiple ships for the same aircraft. Totaling these claims gives a figure of 13 aircraft shot down by anti-aircraft fire out of a total of 43 lost that, 33 of which to enemy fire.

The fighters that were involved in the combat over the *Lexington* were really involved in several complex and convoluted air combats that were typical of this battle but require to much explanation to go into detail here. Nevertheless, a brief summary will be attempted. Initially after the dive-bombing attack of Takahashi there were several dogfights between the defending Wildcats and Dauntlesses and the Zeros supporting the Japanese attack. The Americans had their Combat Air

USS *Lexington* from *Yorktown*, whose SBDs and F4Fs are preparing to take off. This photograph was taken early on the 8th.

Repulse of the Japanese air attack on Admiral Crace's Task Force 44 on May 7. The aircraft are "Nell" bombers (Mitsubishi G3Ms) from Rabaul (see pages 50–51)—the same type of aircraft that sank HMS *Repulse* and *Renown* on December 10, 1941. Task Force 44 is proceeding in a lozenge formation: 1. destroyer USS *Perkins*; 2. destroyer USS *Farragut*; 3. cruiser RAN *Australia*; 4. destroyer USS *Walke*; 5. cruiser RAN *Hobart*; 6. cruiser USS *Chicago*.

The torpedo attack on TF17, 1118–1121hrs, May 8, by Nakajima B5M Kates carrying torpedoes. During the attack *Lexington*'s port side is hit twice (note torpedo runs at lower level).

1. DD-349 USS *Dewey*.
2. DD-417 USS *Morris*.
3. CA-36 USS *Minneapolis*.
4. CV-2 *Lexington*.
5. CA-32 USS *New Orleans*.
6. DD-411 USS *Anderson*.
7. DD-360 USS *Phelps*.
8. CA-27 USS *Chester*.
9. DD-355 USS *Aylwin*.
10. CA-34 USS *Astoria* .
11. CV-5 *Yorktown*.
12. DD-414 USS *Russell*.
13. CA-33 USS *Portland*.
14. DD-412 USS *Hammann*.

Patrol in place and had an anti-torpedo plane patrol prepared for that eventuality. The Americans then set upon the returning bombers and fighters. These combats ranged from low-level attacks to the north of the task force to encounters at medium and high altitudes as well. This included aircraft from the fighter groups and a large number (probably as many as 15) of the bombers from the *Lexington*. Because the sky was thick with fighters and bombers it was obviously difficult to tell friend from foe and unfortunate pilots such as Lt. R Hale, who tried to land back on board the *Lexington* after he had been shot up by the Japanese, were lost to friendly fire. American gunners attacked his aircraft when he tried to land and the crew was killed. The aerial combat was vicious and confused, and it is incredible that the Dauntless pilots attempted to engage the Zeros from the *Shokaku* on equal terms. Hata and Izawa claim that Lt. Hoashi and nine fighters shot down 30 aircraft.

The *Zuikaku* group of fighters under Lt. Yuzo was also taking on the Americans under Lt. Cmdr. J. H. Flatley. There were four Americans and nine (some historians say ten) Japanese and at this point it seems that Flatley was flying at about 10,000ft. His division was at the rear of the Task Force and was apparently unoccupied. This is interesting as it highlights the fact that the fighter direction officer was overwhelmed by the amount of activity in the area and therefore on the radar. This would explain the difficulty found by the air controllers, whose screens were full of contacts not all of who could be identified. Not all the American aircraft had some form of IFF (Identification Friend or Foe) equipment and therefore in the middle of a fast moving battle such as this it would be almost impossible to tell which side they were on.

Left and Below: *Lexington* and her destroyer escorts during the battle.

Below Left: Toward dusk on May 8 *Lexington*'s crew abandons ship. In the smoke on port side a destroyer helps to take off the crew. At 1800hrs USS *Phelps* torpedoed the wreck and *Lexington* sank. Just over 200 men died during the fight, but 2,735 officers and men were saved.

Main Photo: *Lexington* enduring a dive-bomber attack around noon, May 8.

Opposite, Above: AA fire downed this attacker, but …

Opposite, Below: … another takes its place. *Lexington* was attacked by nearly 70 aircraft from *Shokaku* and *Zuikaku* on May 8.

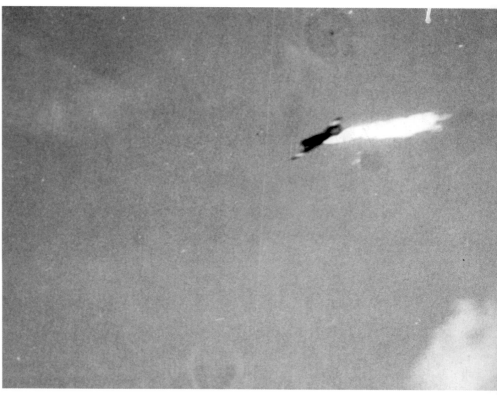

ABOVE: The flightdeck of USS *Lexington* at 1500hrs on May 8. Fires burning below decks cause the smoke to rise. At the front are F4F.3 Wildcats; further back SBD Scout bombers and TBD.1 torpedo bombers.

LEFT: *Lexington*'s anti-aircraft gunners did their best but still could not stop torpedo and bomb hits.

OPPOSITE, ABOVE: Japanese aircraft in the sky above *Lexington*.

OPPOSITE, BELOW: *Lexington* lists and burns after the attack.

Aftermath

The Japanese did not invade Port Moresby, Inoue delayed the advance through the Jomard Passage for a further 48 hours, by which time the main battle had taken place. The *Shokaku* was ordered back to Truk in the Caroline Islands for repairs. In fact she had been severely damaged by American attacks and it was not until she was halfway home and many of her plates began to loosen that the crew began to realize the serious extent of the damage. In the event it would take far longer to repair her than any one had foreseen. Takagi was ordered to return to Truk on May 8 and Operation MO was again postponed until July 3. This decision did not remain in place very long as soon as Adm. Yamamoto got to hear of it and ordered the ships to change course. He countermanded Inoue's order and Takagi was sent south again to look for the elusive Allies. By this time Crace's force had long departed southward. Takagi's force carried out the order at 0200hrs on May 9 and began to zigzag in search of the Allies. They were joined by Goto's force the following day. It was all in vain and no sign of Allied shipping could be found. Yamamoto must have realized the moment had passed as he confirmed a further order of May 11 seeking a general withdrawal and the striking force once again headed back to Truk. Inoue had been particularly concerned when the Tulagi group was attacked on May 10 by the American submarine *S42* and Shiwa's ship, the *Okinoshima*, was sunk. Inoue immediately cancelled operations until it could be proved that U.S. submarines were not a significant threat. The final straw came with the arrival of the *Enterprise* and *Hornet* after Nimitz sent them to the area. They were spotted by the Japanese east of the Solomon Islands and added a new and powerful dimension to the American naval force in the region. On top of the submarine attack the Japanese sought to withdraw to their bases.

What of the Americans? On May 11 they had already decided to split into two groups: the cruisers headed for Nouméa on New Caledonia while the *Yorktown* and her escort headed for Tongatabu in the Tonga Islands for replenishment and repairs. The trials and tribulations of the crew of the *Neosho* as she tried to stay afloat were horrendous. She did not sink after her attack but her rudder was jammed and she was unable to steer and so drifted on the sea currents. For four or so days the hundred odd men on board had put out her fires and hoped that search planes sent out to look for them would detect them.

In fact search planes had been sent out but eventually it was the destroyer *Henley* that was specifically ordered to find the tanker by Admiral Leary. On May 11 a Catalina flying boat did spot the ship and directed the destroyer onto her. After removing the crew the ship was torpedoed and the search continued until May 12 for other survivors. No more were found and the ship left the area and sailed to Brisbane, Australia. Unfortunately they had missed survivors through looking in the wrong place. On May 14 the destroyer *Helm* discovered four men in one of *Neosho*'s rafts that had been on the open ocean for seven days. The two extra carriers, the *Enterprise* and the *Hornet*, that Nimitz had sent to the Coral Sea arrived were recalled immediately to take part in the Battle of Midway.

ABOVE RIGHT: **Following the Battle of the Coral Sea, the British supply ship *Merkur*, with destroyers, cruisers and auxiliary vessels, enters Nouméa Harbor, New Caledonia.**

RIGHT: **An SBD takes off from *Enterprise*, May 12. Note the F4F "dud" with folded wings at left.**

Left and Far Left: *Kikuzuki*, a Mutsuki-class destroyer, was sunk by aircraft from *Yorktown* on May 4 during the Japanese assault on Tulagi. Later in the war, during mid-1943, the *Kikuzuki* was salvaged by the U.S. Navy for intelligence purposes. Subsequently she was moved to Purvis Bay where she remains to this day.

Below: *Yorktown* returns to Pearl Harbor after the battle. Amazingly, the refit she is about to undergo (she will enter drydock on May 27) will take place quickly enough—within three days—to allow CV-5 to be able to take part in the battle of Midway on June 4–5. This helped even the odds, as otherwise only *Hornet* and *Enterprise* would have had to face *Akagi*, *Hiryu*, *Kaga* and *Soryu*. *Yorktown* would not survive Midway, but the battle would be won.

These photographs show USS *Lexington* burning, survivors gathering on the flightdeck, and clambering aboard a rescuing destroyer on May 8. The name Lexington did not die with CV-2. Essex-class carrier CV-16 USS *Cabot* was renamed *Lexington* and went on to survive a torpedoing off Kwajalein in December 1943 and a kamikaze attack in 1944.

Analysis

Historians love to get into the technical minutiae about the differences between equipment and the relative benefits and disadvantages derived from it. In a battle such as this where neither side had any previous experience it can be particulary relevant. Though time and again it is clear that the morale and experience of individual sailors and airmen can be critical to the outcome of a battle. At the Battle of the Coral Sea the Americans had the advantage of radar and the identification friend-or-foe device (or Zed Baker homing unit), whilst the Japanese had a greater proportion of fighters and bombers. The Japanese also had more battle experience and their morale was high. But the Americans appeared to have learned quickly from their mistakes and were more flexible. The Japanese worked to very complicated and intricate plans and once the Americans did not do what was expected of them they were nonplussed, whereas the Americans were more able to adapt and respond to the changing situation. The old maxim that any military plan only survives until first contact with the enemy is absolutely true. The main offensive weapon of both sides in this battle was the aircraft. We have already seen that Japanese fighters were more maneuverable and faster and that their dive-bombers were of higher quality. Yet the Japanese fighter pilots did not decimate the Americans, as one would expect considering the supposed inferiority of their aircraft. It has to be said that American aircraft were robust and reliable and could take a great deal of punishment, a decided factor in their sustainability during this battle. The Japanese aircraft also appeared too vulnerable to direct hits from anti-aircraft fire.

There are a number of key moments that deserve analysis here:

Did Admiral Hara's lack of fighter cover for the dusk attack on the May 7 reduce his fighting capacity? The fail-ure of Admiral Hara to provide fighter cover for his aircraft on the dusk attack of May 7 meant that he wasted an opportunity to destroy American carriers when with fighter cover it may well have been possible. The loss of nine planes may not seem like much out of the possible number available but each time a failure like this occurred the numbers were whittled down, not to mention the vast quantities of fuel and ammunition wasted and this attack does come across as something of a gamble. However, both sides could be accused of gambling and the attack on the *Shoho* and the attacks on the *Neosho* and *Sims* were both wasted efforts when one considers what the ultimate prize could have been.

The confusion between Fitch and Fletcher when refueling between May 1 and 4 has been pointed out as a mistake that cost the Americans the element of surprise. Both Fletcher and Fitch have been accused of not keeping communication channels open during the refueling session on May 4. Fitch took much longer than Fletcher and the Americans lost a day because Fletcher thought Fitch was refueling when in fact he had finished on the 3 May. This had a direct effect on Fletcher's response to the attack on Tulagi forcing him to use the *Yorktown* independently. Had he had the support of the *Lexington* as well and waited for the opportune moment then it may well have been that the surprise experienced by the Japanese at the Tulagi attack would have been replicated by the whole Japanese Fleet.

The lack of air cover for the *Lexington* on May 8 and the poor fighter direction has also been considered as an American failing and there were vocal minority who blamed

LEFT: Japanese aircrew losses at the battles of the Coral Sea and Midway deprived them of some of their most experienced aviators. Losses that were to haunt the Imperial Japanese Navy for the remainder of the war.

it for the loss of the ship. In the report produced by U.S. Naval Intelligence on the battle much is made of the fighter direction during May 8 and Fighter Direction Officer is roundly criticized for not having planned for such an eventuality and allowing the event to happen. As has been seen the planes were low on fuel and that was one of the reasons why the Combat Air Patrol could not be vectored out to the attacking Japanese bombers—they were forced to stay near their mother ship.

This was a battle that was entirely new. Commanders can be forgiven for reacting in any way. The benefit of hindsight shows us that mistakes were made but in reality this takes in little account of the stress that commanders were under, failures in communication and the general fog of war. Tactically the Japanese destroyed a large American carrier and damaged another one. This did not actually affect the ability of the United States to wage naval war, so strategically they could live with the outcome. The Japanese lost an escort carrier and many aircraft. More importantly they lost many experienced pilots and sailors. The more their elite formations were broken up or diluted, the easier it became for the U.S. forces to grind them down.

Many commentators identify this battle as inconclusive. It is the opinion of this author that it was not so. The Japanese losses—of ships and, more importantly, experienced men—and the experience and expertise gained by the U.S. forces, provided, I believe, the first major United States' victory of the Pacific War.

Summary of Japanese losses

Ships sunk	Date
1 carrier—Shoho	May 7
1 light cruiser	May 7
2 destroyers	May 4
1 cargo ship or transport	May 4
4 gunboats	May 4

Ships damaged	Date
1 carrier—Shokaku	May 8
1 aircraft tender	May 4

Aircraft destroyed	Date
33 fighters	May 7 and 8
3 four-engined patrol bombers	May 5, 7, and 8
5 floatplanes	May 4
16 dive-bombers	May 7 and 8
17 torpedo planes	May 7 and 8
30 planes aboard Shoho	

Summary of U.S. losses

Ships sunk	Date
1 carrier—Lexington	May 8
1 oiler—Neosho	May 7
1 destroyer—Sims	May 7

Ships damaged:	Date
1 carrier—Yorktown	May 8

Aircraft destroyed:	Date
15 Lexington planes in combat	May 7 and 8
35 Lexington planes with ship	May 8
16 Yorktown planes in combat	May 4, 7, and 8

Personnel losses were estimated at 543; the enemy's at anywhere from 2,000 to 5,000.

References

the
dauntless
dive bomber
of world war two
by barrett tillman

THE
FIRST
TEAM

Pacific Naval Air Combat
from Pearl Harbor to Midway

JOHN B. LUNDSTROM

Bibliography

Books

Belote, James H., and Belote, William M., *Titans of the Seas: The Development and Operations of Japanese and American Carrier Task Forces During World War II.* New York: Harper & Row, 1975.
A useful description of the design, deployment and operational history of carrier task forces, one of the most important naval developments of World War II.

Coffey, Thomas M., *Imperial Tragedy: Japan in World War II, the First Days and the Last.* New York: World Pub. Co. 1970.
As the title suggests, this book concentrates on the very early events of the war, predominately Pearl Harbor, and the final days. It is particularly good on the Japanese perspective.

Costello, John, *The Pacific War.* New York: Rawson, Wade, 1981.
A very good single-volume history of the entire war in the Pacific.

Cressman, Robert, *That Gallant Ship: USS Yorktown (CV-5).* Missoula, Mont.: Pictorial Histories Pub. Co. 1985.
Covers the history of the *Yorktown* through the early battles of the Pacific War to her demise at the Battle of Midway.

Dull, Paul S., *A Battle History of The Imperial Japanese Navy 1941–1945.* Annapolis: Naval Institute Press, 1978.
An interesting book composed with the use of previously unknown Japanese documents.

Dunnigan, J. F., and Nofi, A. A., *Victory at Sea, World War Two in the Pacific.* New York: William Morrow and Co., 1995.
This book has so much information on all aspects of

the war in the Pacific that it is difficult to be objective about it. Many of the facts and figures used to illustrate logistic requirements and supplies come from here and I would recommend it to anyone who requires a complete overview of the war backed up by significant data.

Hata, Ikuhiko, and Izawa, Yasuho, *Japanese Naval Aces and Fighter Units in World War II*. Annapolis: Naval Institute Press, 1989.
An insight into the stories of Japanese aviators and their units. The claims of kills are somewhat exaggerated but this book represents a very welcome Japanese point of view and is full of interesting insights into the Japanese naval air arm.

Howarth, Stephen, *Morning Glory, A History of The Imperial Japanese Navy*. London: Hamish Hamilton, 1983.
A general history of the Imperial Japanese Navy from its inception to its defeat.

Johnson, Stanley, *Queen of the Flat Tops—The USS Lexington and the Coral Sea Battle*. New York: Doubleday, 1979.
Contains many quotations from the men who were there and newspaper reports that were written at the time.

Lindley, John M. *Carrier Victory: The Air War in the Pacific*. New York: Dutton, 1951.
A Well illustrated, though somewhat dated, account of World War II in the Pacific.

Lundstrom, John B. *The First South Pacific Campaign: Pacific Fleet Strategy, December 1941–June 1942*. Annapolis: Naval Institute Press, 1976
Covers the early campaigns of the war from January 42–June 1942. it is particularly good on strategy.

Lundstrom, John B. *The first team. Pacific naval air combat from Pearl Harbor to Midway*. Annapolis: Naval Institute Press, 1976.
An excellent, detailed view of American naval aviation exploits in the Pacific. The detail is astounding and although it concentrates mainly on the aircraft it gives a brilliant insight into the way in which aircraft were handled during the early phases of the conflict. Just about the best combat reference of American naval aircraft activities in the early part of the war.

Millot, Bernard, *The Battle of the Coral Sea*. Sea Battles in Close Up, No. 12. Annapolis: Naval Institute Press, 1974.
A comprehensive account of the battle with the emphasis on the air encounters.

Morison, Samuel, *History of United States Naval Operations in World War II*. Boston: Little Brown and Co., 1947–62.
XV volumes.
The official history of the U.S. Navy and very readable. A starting point for those interested in the Pacific War.

Naval Intelligence Combat Reports. Navy Department, Office of Naval Intelligence: Washington, D.C. 1943.
Probably the best primary source of information with detailed comments of officers and ratings during the battle. It was written in 1943 after all the information had been assimilated and not only gives comments but also analysis of the shortcomings of the U.S. Navy. If there were a Japanese version of this document it would make interesting reading.

Smith, Peter C., *Impact! The Dive Bomber Pilots speak*. New York: William Kimber and Co., 1981.
This general title covers the dive-bomber pilots from all the combatant countries of World War II and has some very good first-hand accounts of the Pacific War.

Spector, Ronald H., *Eagle against the Sun*. New York: Free Press, 1984.
Spector's gargantuan work on the Japanese American war has covered all aspects of the political and military spectrum.

Tillman, Barret, *The Dauntless dive-bomber of WW2*. Annapolis: Naval Institute Press, 1976.
A very good analysis of this aircraft with insight into how it was used and all its variants.

The Battle of the Coral Sea Conference Proceedings 1992. Australian National Maritime Museum.
A rare and unusual perspective from several contributors but especially the Japanese contribution, which gives an interesting military perspective as to why the Japanese may have thought the Coral Sea was a failure.

The Japanese Navy in World War II. With an introduction and commentary by Raymond G. O'Connor. Annapolis: U.S. Naval Institute, 1969.
An anthology of articles by former officers of the Imperial Japanese Navy and Air Defense Force, originally published in the U.S. Naval Institute *Proceedings*.

Van der Vat, Dan. *The Pacific Campaign: World War II, the U.S.–Japanese Naval War, 1941–1945*. New York: Simon & Schuster, 1991.
Although limited by being only 400 pages long this is a good single-volume account of the war in the Pacific and a useful starting point.

Magazines

Warship Journal

This long-established journal contains many excellent articles on the navies of both sides. Of particular interest are:

Itani, Jiro, Legerer, Hans, and Takahara, Tomoko Rehm, "Anti-aircraft Gunnery in the Imperial Japanese Navy"
Friedman, Norman, "The 5-inch 38-calibre gun"

Websites

There are many websites relating to the Battle of the Coral Sea but they are often general or concentrate on the whole Pacific War. The Naval Historical Center, http://www.history.navy.mil/index.html, is probably the best and is more of an online museum giving accounts, photographs and biographies with the facility to contact them if further information is required. The following are also of interest:

http://navalhistory.flixco.info/—A naval history of World War II, with detailed coverage of ships, weapons and technical data.

http://www.bluejackets.com—A great site dedicated to the U.S. Navy with all sorts of information from technical descriptions to people.

http://www.combinedfleet.com—Has a really good section on the Japanese Navy although some parts are incomplete. It also has some very nice images of IJN ships.

http://home.vicnet.net.au/~gcasey/welcome.html—Coral Sea references from the point of view of Gavan Casey, including some good references for Australian ships and some firsthand accounts.

http://www.gunplot.net—Another Australian site with its own unique perspective.

http://www.warship.get.net.pl/—A more general Polish site dealing with warship history. It has excellent sections dealing with the vessels used in the Pacific War.